INVASIONS USA

INVASIONS USA

The Essential Science Fiction Films of the 1950s

Michael Bliss

ROWMAN & LITTLEFIELD
Lanham • Boulder • New York • London

Published by Rowman & Littlefield
A wholly owned subsidiary of The Rowman & Littlefield Publishing Group, Inc.
4501 Forbes Boulevard, Suite 200, Lanham, Maryland 20706
www.rowman.com

16 Carlisle Street, London W1D 3BT, United Kingdom

British Library Cataloguing in Publication Information Available

Library of Congress Cataloging-in-Publication Data

Bliss, Michael, 1947–
Invasions USA : the essential science fiction films of the 1950s / Michael Bliss
p. cm.
Includes bibliographical references and index.
Includes filmography.
ISBN 978-1-4422-3651-6 (hardback : alk. paper) — ISBN 978-1-4422-3652-3 (ebook) 1. Science
fiction films—United States—History and criticism. 2. Motion pictures—United States—History—
20th century. I. Title.
PN1995.9.S26B55 2014
791.43'615—dc23
2014014308

Printed in the United States of America

For Tony Colaianne

CONTENTS

INTRODUCTION

America under the Alien Microscope

> But there were too many points at which the other self could invade the self he wanted to preserve, and there were too many forms of invasion. . . —Patricia Highsmith, *Strangers on a Train*

A young boy has nightmares in which his parents and other people are transformed into alien-controlled automatons. A spaceship crashes into the Arctic ice and out of it emerges a creature that thrives on blood. The day before her marriage, a young woman's fiancé is abducted by aliens and replaced by an emotionless double. A flying saucer lands in Washington, D.C. One of its occupants is an extraterrestrial who warns humans that if they don't suppress their militaristic aggressiveness their planet will be destroyed. And in a small California town, alien duplicates that seem bent on taking over the planet begin to proliferate.

Those are just some of the events that occur in this book's films. All of these films are from the 1950s. And in one way or another, all of them involve some sort of invasion. Interestingly, among the 182 science fiction films produced in the United States between 1950 and 1959, twenty were concerned with the notion of an invasion.[1] Within this group is a fascinating subset of eleven films that do more than portray an invasion, but also use the invasions as metaphors for assaults against the integrity of various things such as the self, marriage, and notions involving the supremacy of the human race. The invasion may be real, as it is in *The Day the Earth Stood Still* and *The War of the Worlds*. It may be imagined, as it is in *Invaders from Mars*. It may even be the result of a mental break-down, as seems to be the case in *Invasion of the Body Snatchers*. Real or not, all of these massive disturbances of the status quo tell us the same thing: in the 1950s, many Americans felt that things in their world weren't quite right. And as often happens, this sense of unease was expressed in the country's art. These films are part of that great tradition.

Previous books on 1950s American science fiction films have offered explanations for why many of these films tell the same type of story. The answers offered in some of these books is that these films are about fear of either Communist takeover or nuclear war.[2] But these explanations seem too pat, too conventional, to be entire-ly convincing. The notion of Communist infiltration was predomi-nantly a fiction used by American politicians for their own gain, and most Americans knew it. True, there was a risk of nuclear war in the 1950s but again, it was a fear whose intensity was exaggerat-ed by politicians for their own gain. Instead, it seems to me that the very real anxieties dramatized in these films involve fears that come from a region more personal than political. They come from the depths of human psychology. And what they tell us is that the supposedly placid 1950s were haunted by the stuff of nightmares.

As might be expected, the ends of many of these films are not reassuring. *Invaders from Mars'* David and *Invasion of the Body Snatchers'* Miles seem trapped within nightmares. Despite *The Day the Earth Stood Still's* warning about impending doom, it seems unlikely that humans will suppress their aggressiveness. It's doubt-ful that the central marriage in *I Married a Monster from Outer Space* will ever achieve some sort of normalcy. Nor does it seem likely that the primary relationships in *Kronos* and *The Thing from Another World* are going to be productive ones. Indeed, with the exception of *The Incredible Shrinking Man*, little hope is held out for these films' characters at each film's conclusion. TV situation comedies in the 1950s may have been full of happy families and smiling couples, but most of the people in these films are already well on their way to despair. The question is, of course, which set of stories was telling us the truth?

There's no doubt as to how all but one of the films discussed herein would answer that question. With the exception of the remarkably traditional view of American life taken in George Pal's movies, the films that I've chosen to discuss are notable for being harshly critical of the way that Americans were living in the 1950s. Of all the films discussed in this book, director Robert Wise's *The Day the Earth Stood Still* is both the most restrained and the most critical of the way that not only Americans but many nations throughout the world were conducting their affairs. While the film's major critique is directed against militarism, there's no denying that *Day* is really about the virtually unchecked aggressiveness that can be found among many individuals. In fact, it could be argued that the film views political behavior as nothing more than an extension of how individuals treat each other. With this view in mind, things are no better in some of this book's other films. The male leads in *Kronos* and *The Thing from Another World* are misogynistic. The harsh treatment that *I Married*'s Marge undergoes at the hands of her alien double husband is a reflection of the way that many Earth men behave toward their wives and girlfriends. The same can be said for the sexist attitude of *Invasion*'s Miles and *Shrinking Man*'s Scott. Ironically, the most "human," caring male figure in any of these films is an alien: *Day*'s Klaatu, who expresses his respect and affection for a woman in a much more meaningful way than do any of the men in this book's other films.

Klaatu is significant in another respect. He's one of the array of intergalactic visitors that populate these films, all of whom are in the classic Freudian sense uncanny in that they're strange and yet familiar at the same time.[3] We experience them as just different enough from the norm to attract attention, yet they're also recognizable enough with regard to what they tell us about ourselves to make us appreciate how alien from our true natures many of us have become. As Freud notes,

> [The] uncanny is in reality nothing new or alien, but something which is familiar and old—established in the mind and which has become alienated from it only through the process of repression.[4]

In various ways, these films want us not only to take a close, virtually microscopic look at ourselves (as though from an alien point of view) but to reform our behavior, which means that not only do the films believe that humans need to change, they also believe that somehow, humans are capable of doing so. All of these films hope to influence us positively. They aim to do so by taking advantage of one of the ways that we respond to the uncanny.

If it's true that what seems unfamiliar can many times seem familiar, it's equally true that the familiar can seem strange. The creation of the latter effect is one of these films' main purposes. For example, the point of Klaatu's mission to Earth is to get humans to recognize what they should have already known but, for various self-serving reasons, have repressed: that their aggressiveness is a threat to the planet's continued existence, if not from an alien attack then from the consequences of human behavior. If Klaatu's arrival on Earth seems strange to humans, one of its consequences may be that what seems familiar to humans, in this case our hostility, may as a result of the strange nature of the alien and robot's presence start to unhinge us from the usual way of viewing ourselves and move us toward a vantage point distant enough from the norm so that, perhaps for the first time in a long while, we see ourselves as though from the perspective of something unusual, something strange—in other words, something alien. What we discover is that what's really strange in these films isn't the otherworldly beings that appear in them but us, who are the real aliens.

Unfortunately, in a maddeningly paradoxical fashion, given the way that most of them conclude, these films are not optimistic about humans' capability for change. At the end of their respective films, *Invaders'* David relapses into his endless loop nightmare and *Invasion's* Miles descends into complete madness. Despite the quite reasonable warning toward the beginning of *The Day the Earth Stood Still*, if we're to judge by subsequent events, many of the planet's inhabitants are not interested in suppressing their aggression. *I Married's* Marge is, and always will be, married to an alien, while the male leads in *Kronos* and *The Thing* fall into conventional relationships that are just as entrapping as the one that helped drive *Invasion's* Miles to madness. The only invasions that end positively are those in *The Incredible Shrinking Man* and *The War of the Worlds*, although it should be noted that the latter film's triumphant ending has nothing to do with human effort and everything to do with an indifferent force.

The point of these films (even *The War of the Worlds*, which expresses its values through clichés) is to refamiliarize us with the best impulses that humans have, among them love, compassion, forgiveness, and trust, qualities diametrically opposed to those that critics often associate with these films' ambience. The films encourage us to move toward that state of loving acceptance achieved by the main character, Scott Carey, at the end of *The Incredible Shrinking Man*. Alone, near naked, Scott realizes that he is a small part of some great plan. After all the duplicity, deception, and madness in the previous films, we come at the end of this book to a film that promotes an understanding and acceptance so powerful that they're indistinguishable from love.

The book's first chapter deals with a film that provides a fine gateway into 1950s American science fiction films: director William Cameron Menzies's *Invaders from Mars*. On the surface, this film is about a young boy's dream about Martians invading his hometown and taking control of his parents and other people. Examined more closely, though, the film is also a chilling depiction of a disturbed psychology that reflects the type of fears caused by common stresses within the typical American family and American culture. More than a dream (from which, in this chapter's view, the sleeper never wakes), young David's nighttime fantasy about malicious parents and evil children is revealed to be a very prevalent, disturbing reality in 1950s America.

Chapter 2 discusses director Don Siegel's *Invasion of the Body Snatchers*, which is widely considered the prototypical 1950s science fiction film. Although Siegel said many times that he wasn't making a metaphor about fears of Communism, many people still treat the film as though he had. In this book's view, Siegel's film about a small California town invaded by pods that replicate and take over humans is mostly about the problems associated with insular small-town American life, a theme dramatically portrayed in what the chapter argues is its major precursor: Sinclair Lewis's novel *Main Street*. In this view, the film's story about an alien invasion is actually a coherent paranoid fantasy spun by a professional man who's been driven mad by fears of his ex-girlfriend's return to town and his anger at how trapped he is within not only his hometown but his own swirling series of personal anxieties. The chapter supports its approach to the film by extensively discussing the screenplay's source: Jack Finney's novel *The Body Snatchers*, which is usually overlooked in writing on the film.

Chapter 3 focuses on *The Day the Earth Stood Still*, a cautionary story about apocalypse that remains one of the most intelligent and emotionally effective arguments against humans' tendency to want to destroy themselves that has ever been committed to film. Although scriptwriter Edmund North wrote into the film hints that its alien invader Klaatu is also a Jesus figure, the real significance of the film is not only its decidedly antiwar stance (quite unpopular when the film was released) but its insistence that humans take a long, hard look at themselves and their tendency to harm not only themselves but others with their selfish politics and personal behavior.

The notion of self-centeredness is also present in *It Came from Outer Space*, which is discussed in chapter 4. The film's criticism of prejudice and xenophobia, quite daring for the period in which it was made, has often been overlooked in favor of attention to its visuals, which were enhanced by the film's being shot in 3-D. Yet *It Came*'s greatest dimensionality derives from its intelligent script, which sensitively metaphorizes racial and cultural bigotry.

Very few films have a title as intriguing as director Gene Fowler Jr.'s *I Married a Monster from Outer Space*, which is discussed in chapter 5. This film is a commentary on not only the all-too-familiar story of learning too late what your partner in a romantic relationship is really like but on the assumptions that many couples make about marriage and sex. *I Married* shows us that for many women, marriage is a powerfully alienating psychological, emotional, and physical nightmare from which they feel that they cannot escape.

Chapter 6 discusses *Kronos* and *The Thing from Another World*. Although at first glance the films seem unrelated, a strong case can be made for how both films about an alien invader intent on world domination are subtle metaphors for American men's fear of women. The alien robot Kronos intends to drain Earth of all its power. The film's lead scientist fears that his girlfriend intends to drain him of his energy by trapping him into a marriage. From the viewpoint of *The Thing*'s main character, a promiscuous air force captain, his onetime girlfriend (like the film's alien invader) is a powerful vampiric force who in his view intends to rob him of his life's blood: his sexual freedom. Each film turns out to be a depiction of how, without acknowledging it, American men in the 1950s continued a long tradition (depicted in classic American literature such as Hawthorne's "Young Goodman Brown" and Twain's *Adventures of Huckleberry Finn*) of some men's desire to escape from what they regard as the entrapments of domesticity.

Producer George Pal's film *The War of the Worlds*, which is covered in chapter 7, seems like a straightforward dramatization of H. G. Wells's novel, but when it's considered along with Pal's biography (he was a refugee from Nazism) and some of his other 1950s science fiction films (e.g., *Conquest of Space* and *When Worlds Collide*), it can also be read as a story that not only depicts a threat to planetary integrity but a conflict involving a clash of different ideas about government, all of them influenced by Pal's Catholic background. Pal brought with him to the United States a fear of totalitarianism so strong that his alternative was a view of politics so wholesome that in its own way was just as exaggerated as what he was reacting against.

The book concludes with a discussion of *The Incredible Shrinking Man*, a film about a young man invaded by alien particles that cause him to shrink to virtual nothingness. Director Jack Arnold's film is not only a special effects tour de force but a deeply introspective study of how various forms of diminishment—physical, emotional, sexual, and psychological—were endemic to many American men in the 1950s. Scott Carey's small size is a metaphor for his tiny sense of self-worth but at the film's end, after a process toward acceptance that is deeply spiritual, he reaches a sense of peace that is the highlight of this serious and profound film. Unlike other critical writings on 1950s American science fiction films, this chapter includes extensive discussion of the film's source, Richard Matheson's novel *The Shrinking Man*, and its relation to director Jack Arnold's film.

These films dramatize a spectrum of human emotions that run from terror, despair, rejection, alienation, depression, confusion, and abject fear to the final film discussed, in which all these factors are transcended via a resignation to the divine. This is a truly extraordinary group of films. My hope is that you find as much in them to appreciate as I have.

I

SLEEPWALKING: *INVADERS FROM MARS*

The Sleep of Reason Produces Monsters—title of an etching by
Francisco Goya

In director William Cameron Menzies's *Invaders from Mars*
(1953), the fantastical is in full force. In fact, it has invaded what
many people regard as one of the most intimate parts of their being:
their dreams. But along with the film's depiction of a child's unusual imaginings are the types of rationalizations typically found in the
adult world, in which people analyze events and try to make sense
of what they see. Thus, the fantastical and the rational contend in
the film. And though we're attracted to the film because of how
unusual it is, we're also upset by what it shows us because we
know how significant it is.

Originally conceived in 1949 by Richard Blake (who based his
scenario on a dream experienced by the wife of story treatment
writer John Tucker Battle), *Invaders from Mars* went into production in 1950 but was held back from release until 1953. The film
tells the story of David MacLean (Jimmy Hunt), a young boy who
dreams about a Martian spaceship landing behind his house. The
aliens begin to implant control devices in various humans, David's
parents George and Mary (Leif Erickson and Hillary Brooke)
among them. [1]

Although there's little doubt about which *Invaders'* characters are being controlled by the Martians, the film still has a great deal of indeterminacy in it, in particular with regard to an issue with which David is strongly concerned: trust. Throughout the film, David searches for people who will believe what he tells them about the Martian invasion. The first people whom David speaks to regarding what he thinks that he's seen are his parents, who doubt his story. Perhaps it's because David didn't really expect that his parents would credit his story that he goes on to dream about finding substitutes for them. First, he dreams of a father figure who says that David is "not the type of boy given to imagining things." Then, he dreams an extended series of events that prove to many of the adults around him that this assertion is true.

In David's dream, the father figure is the astronomer Dr. Kelston (Arthur Franz), to whom David ascribes all of the paternal qualities that he desires. In contrast to George MacLean, Kelston doesn't hide the truth about the work at the local rocket plant. Instead, albeit in a somewhat ludicrous way (Kelston focuses a telescope that is meant to observe the cosmos on an area that is at best only a few miles away), he fully reveals it. By contrast, George MacLean tells his wife that what goes on at the rocket plan can't be discussed. (Interestingly, information about the work at the plant has been buried in a manner analogous to the way that the aliens hide beneath the surface of the sand pit behind the MacLeans' house.) What kind of information regarding the facility is being hidden? First, that there may be aliens near the rocket project, and second, that the scientists are building an atomic-powered rocket. Apparently, this project has prompted the Martian invasion. Army sergeant Rinaldi, who's being controlled by the Martians, says that the Martians fear that rockets from Earth will somehow threaten the rockets in which many of the Martians live, the surface of their planet having become uninhabitable. As in *The Day the Earth Stood Still, Invaders'* aliens don't trust humans when it comes to how advanced technology is used. The fact that distrust of how scientific advancements are used is part of the dream of a young boy who wants to be a scientist tells us how deeply conflicted David is.

Where Kelston is not only scientifically knowledgeable but paternal, physician Dr. Pat Blake (Helena Carter) combines medical knowledge with a maternal aspect. Once David's skepticism concerning Dr. Blake is allayed (he examines the back of her neck, the area where the Martians implant control devices), it is replaced by candor and an immediate emotional attraction. Blake's obvious compassion is reflected in the colors that she wears. Her white dress hints at the purity of her motives. The red handkerchief in her breast pocket suggests both warmth and passion.[2] This attractive woman offers not only protective intervention (she refuses to let David's parents take him home from the police station, claiming that he has symptoms of polio) but also the potential for the kind of love that David possibly wants from his mother, whom he probably views as representative of all women. Dr. Blake becomes not just a confidante and protector but a focal point for David's nascent sexual feelings, which are expressed during the scene in which the unconscious Blake is lying on a table while an alien probe moves ever closer to her, threatening penetration. Since the film suggests some romantic interest between Kelston and Blake, and lets us know that David is an aspiring astronomer, it's hinted that David wants to assume not only Kelston's professional role but his sexual one as well.

Kelston and Blake, who assume the function of David's surrogate parents, are conceived of as scientific professionals, which tells us a great deal about what David thinks of his real parents. Since the idealized parents are respectively an astronomer (a professional role to which David aspires)[3] and an M.D. (ideally, a trusted advisor), while the real parents are a research engineer with indeterminate duties and a temperamentally mercurial housewife, both of whom are eventually viewed as untrustworthy, we can assume that David has a low regard for his parents' "real-life" status.[4] The boy seems to value them on a personal level but doesn't think much of them on a professional one—a sign of his deeply conflicted nature.

Judging from his dream, David's anxiety about his home life has percolated down into his subconscious. David fears this realm, partially because he wishes to avoid what it has to tell him about his true feelings about science, scientific progress, and his parents and associates. But nothing that is repressed remains that way. As Freud notes in his essay "The Uncanny,"

> If psycho-analytic theory is correct in maintaining that every affect belonging to an emotional impulse, whatever its kind, is transformed, if it is repressed, into anxiety, then among instances of frightening things there must be one class in which the frightening element can be shown to be something repressed which *recurs*.[5]

David yearns to live in a world in which he is protected by his parents. When David's alarm clock inadvertently wakes them early one morning (he wants to get up early to see a special celestial event), his father, who is not only caring enough to share his son's interests but childlike enough to be an avid participant in one of them, initially responds in an understanding fashion. George and David sit on the boy's bedroom floor and peer through his telescope. Both of them simultaneously experience the joy of discovery. That George and David's closeness is transmuted in David's dream into not just alienation but intimidation and physical violence indicates what a horror David's dream world is.

Even in David's (supposed) waking life, his mother is somewhat stern. Annoyed at being awakened, Mary first insists that David go back to bed. She goes on to state that now that she's been disturbed, her husband will have to make his own (and David's?) breakfast while she goes back to sleep. Essentially, she is punishing her

husband and son for their devotion to astronomy. This condemnation of one of David's prime concerns is dramatized in the boy's
dream in which, of the two transformed parents, the mother becomes the more ominous. George MacLean may strike his son, but
Mary MacLean is sinister, a quality seen quite clearly in the police
station scene when, in a tight close-up, she looks unfeelingly into
the camera and ominously arches her eyebrow. [6]

The parents' transformation is dramatic. The loving, supportive
father of the film's beginning becomes an intolerant, overly defensive man who is easily angered and extremely secretive about his
work. The mother becomes a frightening figure of unemotionality,
an "Other" dressed in black who has been robotized into precisely
the kind of woman that her altered husband wants: a machine that
assists him in the Martian plot to take over the world.

Characters from many different professional groups (especially
scientists, the military, and the police) fall under the invaders' control. David's distrust of people is implied by the rapidity of the
transformations. David's sense of how mercurial the world seems
to be is reflected in many of the film's sets, which are either redo-
lent with instability (the shifting sand at the sand pit, the sand pit
fence that is present at one point and gone the next), terror (the
striking emptiness of and exaggerated perspectives in the police
station), or unreality (the patently artificial backdrop behind the
house of David's neighbor Cathy).

The central part of *Invaders'* action takes place between the first
and second times that David's alarm clock goes off. This action is
framed by two events: the action that takes place at the film's
beginning (at 4 a.m., when David first wakes up to look at the stars)
and the action at the film's end, between the time that David supposedly awakes from his dream (4:40 a.m.) and the time that the
film's central action begins to repeat itself (albeit with important
variations that I'll soon discuss). It's tempting to conclude that the
frame's events take place in the real world. It's also tempting to

believe what David's father tells him toward the end of the film's American version: that the preceding action, which begins with David's seeing the alien ship land, has been a dream. However, the film provides ample evidence that even the frame story's events take place in a dream, in which case the film's central action is a dream *within* a dream.

The introduction into David's dream within a dream begins with a flash of lightning and claps of thunder. We see another shot of the clock, which now reads 4:40. Within this dream, time does not progress. Granted, there are events within the dream that occur before others. The Martian ship lands; people are transformed; Dr. Blake, Kelston, and the army become involved. Finally, the Martians are destroyed. What we have here appears to be a normal chronology of events. Yet the film is filled with anomalous images. On the way to the police station, David stops at a grocery store that prominently displays tomatoes in cans that are positioned upside down. And though David speaks to the police chief in his office, the door located to the left of the desk at which the sergeant sits is gone when David's parents come to retrieve him. We can't ascribe these facts to failures in continuity. Menzies is too careful a production designer to overlook such glaring discrepancies.[7] Rather, the upside-down cans suggest that in the world of David's dream, the normal is often inverted, while the disappearance of the door emphasizes that inside the dream realm, things don't just shift position but sometimes completely disappear. The sense of the unreal on the one hand and impermanence on the other give us a powerful appreciation for the enveloping, claustrophobic, disturbing nature of David's tortured psychology.[8]

In its last few shots, *Invaders* reprises the action from the dream's beginning, during which the Martian ship landed and sank below the surface of the sand pit adjacent to David's house.[9] We could conclude that the dream was merely a prescient view of these later events, and that variations between the scenes at the beginning

and end of the film that depict the ship landing (e.g., the di͟
in the sound of the ship and the presence of rain) are mean͟ ͟͟
highlight the distinction between the dream and real worlds. Yet
it's also possible that David never wakes up from his nightmare.

Consider the different sounds that the Martian ship makes.
When landing at the film's beginning, the ship gives off an electronic hum. At the film's end, though, the ship sounds like a prop-
driven airplane. The electronic sound that comes from the ship is
only heard within David's dream within a dream, the part of the
film that takes up the majority of its running time. The sound is
eerie and slightly alien, in keeping with the "Otherness" of this
section's action. In the frame story (which is also a dream), David
has returned to a realm that is only one step removed from his
conscious life. The action at the film's beginning occurs in this
realm, within which David believes that he first wakes up, before
the dream within a dream begins. In this outer dream realm, David
is only slightly removed from the real world. He's in the realm
between sleeping and waking in which one is still aware of certain
impressions from the material world but within which these impressions take on ideational suggestibility, a form of representation
that is predominantly that of the dream realm. Author Celia Green
states that this realm involves what she refers to as a Type 2 false
awakening:

> In this type of false awakening the subject appears to wake up in
> a realistic manner, but to an atmosphere of suspense. These
> experiences vary in respect of the length of time which elapses
> before the subject becomes aware that something unusual is
> happening. His surroundings may appear normal, and he may
> gradually become aware of something uncanny in the atmos-
> phere, and perhaps of unwonted sounds and movements. Or he
> may "awake" immediately to a "stressed" and "stormy" atmos-
> phere. In either case, the end result would appear to be charac-
> terized by feelings of suspense, excitement or apprehension. [10]

It's therefore quite natural that at the film's end, when the Martian ship once again begins to make its descent into the sand pit, it sounds like a conventional airplane. The dreamlike image of the alien ship has been combined with a sound associated with human-created machinery since at this point, David is not only midway between deep and light sleep but midway between his fear that the Martians will once again initiate their invasion and his hope that there is some non-dream realm inhabited by real people within which the Martians can be defeated. Regrettably, given the fact that, as before, the mild dream realm of the frame story will yield to the full dream realm, the same outcome that we've already seen will doubtless occur: David will dream of the invasion, the quelling of the invasion, and the reinitiation of the invasion, an oneiric loop from which he finds it impossible to escape. Because of David's inability to break free from his fears, most of which he has associated with the Martians, the conclusion to which we're led seems inevitable: the Martians, and all that they represent about the dangerous pull of David's phobias, have triumphed.[11]

In David's dream within a dream, George and Mary MacLean lack emotion. This emotionlessness expresses the boy's fear of his parents' affection being withdrawn. Why would a child be so insecure in this regard? One possible reason for this anxiety comes from David's view of what it means to grow up. He wants to be an adult with an adult job yet at the same time seems to worry that maturity will involve the loss of the unconditional love that he idealizes. Deep down, David doesn't want to mature, doesn't want to enter the real world with all of its threats and anxieties. He'd rather remain in his dream world in which, despite all of its terrors, a scenario involving rescue and deliverance plays out. This view would explain why at the end of the film, the dream doubles back on itself. David wants to stay within his dream world, within which he feels safe from the real world's horrors. Unfortunately, David lacks the psychological balance to not only break free of the dream within the dream but of the enclosing, self-perpetuating frame dream as well. On some level, David may feel that his dream, and his dream within the dream, are nightmarish, but as the film's conclusion demonstrates, he feels that the nightmare of the real world into which he will awake is far, far worse. Ultimately, that is the film's real horror.

David's central dream contains elements that he has attempted to forget but which he cannot. In this dream, the small number of (apparently) conscious remnants that we see (e.g., his protesting to Kelston that George and Mary MacLean are nice people) have yielded to the pull of his unconscious promptings, which tell him something that he resists: his parents seem suspiciously dangerous and threatening. The repeated sinkings of people into the Martian-controlled sand pit show us individuals whom David considers good being sucked into the horror world of his subconscious, within which they fall under the Martians' control. The sand pit (and all the terrors that it embodies) is like a dream realm within a dream that is itself enclosed by a dream, another example of the film's technique of embedding concepts within concepts, a form of cocooning whose "shape" parallels that of the swirling openings in the sand that draw people down into the netherworld. [12]

David's nightmare also highlights the filmmakers' view of how deplorable 1950s American culture really is. The boy's life within the frame story seems suspiciously conventional, so much so that the film appears to be telling us that one of the most frightening things in 1950s America is the normality to which it aspires. The crushing, insufferable blandness of the 1950s is merely one of the things from which David desperately tries to escape.

The area around the house in which David and his parents live looks like a wasteland. Its lack of detail is a metaphor for a cultural absence of imagination as well as the presence of deeply disturbing isolation. The house's surroundings symbolize what David believes are adulthood promises (at least, the adulthood that David's parents represent): a place of both terror (forced perspectives, a twisted fence that drops off into a void) and vast emptiness. The houses near David's are no better. Behind Cathy's house is a backdrop on which is painted the view from the back of the house. The colors in the painting are washed out and the image lacks depth (qualities in stark contrast to the deeply saturated colors and exaggerated perspectives in the sand pit area, which is associated with the story of the Martians). The backdrop signifies more than just a failure of the imagination of middle-class Americans, whose comfortable lifestyles are purchased by adopting uniformity and straitened behaviors. It also tells us that, by contrast, the fantastical story of the Martian invasion, for all of its ludicrous aspects, is rich with the colors of inventiveness.

Cathy's setting fire to her parents' house can be seen as an act of protest against American middle-class life. She's attempting to destroy a culture of sameness that wants its children to mature into it. In this regard, what can the Martian invasion be if not the realization of David's wish to destroy his waking life and, despite how horrible it may be, substitute a dream life in which an exciting battle is being waged, and in which he is its hero? Within this dream, he invents dream parents who (in an ironic mirroring of the film's transformation theme) replace his real parents.

There's another anxiety expressed in the dream. Sergeant Rinaldi says of the emotionally indifferent Martian leader that "he is mankind taken to its ultimate form." Apparently, David fears that with increased intelligence comes diminution of emotion, to the point at which, saddled with massive mental acuity, one carries out invasions, abductions, and forced transformations.[13] In essence, David suspects that great intelligence is bought at the price of diminished humanity, a condition characterized by emptiness (the holes in the sand), isolation (the Martian leader's head in a glass sphere), and mindlessness (the Martian mutants).[14]

There are two versions of the film: one American, one British.[15] The American version ends with David's inner dream presumably ending. The army has planted an explosive device in one of the underground chambers that the Martians have dug. While Kelston, Dr. Blake, David, and other characters are running away from the ship's location, David recalls events from the film. We see reprises of David looking at the back of people's necks to see if they've had a Martian control device implanted, of the transformed police captain putting on his hat, of some Martian mutants running through underground chambers, as well as many other shots from scenes in which David doesn't appear. Interspersed with these images are shots that have been printed in reverse, which suggests a rolling back of all of the dream's preceding events, something that comes to fruition toward the end of the film when David awakens from his inner dream and, still dreaming, runs into his parents' bedroom to tell them about the Martian ship, which he's once again just seen land. In their bedroom, David's parents assure him that everything is fine, that all of his fears are based on events that only happened in a dream. In the succeeding scene, David is back in bed. As he had at the inner dream's beginning, David's father bids him good night, a repetition that foreshadows the repetitions to follow. A thunderclap is heard, the Martian saucer is once again sighted, and another thunderclap announces the ship's penetration of the ground's surface. After David "wakes," goes to his bedroom window, and stares out, another thunderclap is heard, after which (in contrast to what happens toward the film's beginning) it begins to rain. As noted earlier, the sound of the ship is now different.

The British censor found the film's dream premise objectionable. In order to obtain censor approval for the film, *Invaders'* producer brought back actors Arthur Franz, Jimmy Hunt, and Helena Carter in order to shoot new footage that was meant to be more comforting to audiences in the United Kingdom.[16] At the end of this version of the film, the Martian ship is not exploded underground (as occurs in the American version). Instead, presumably to affirm that the ship has really been destroyed, we see it take off and blow up in midair. To further make the film more conventional, the flashback images that David sees while he and others are running away from the area where the Martian ship is buried are eliminated.[17] In the most striking change from the film's American version, instead of showing us George MacLean looking down at David in his bed, the British version ends the film with Kelston and Blake taking the roles of David's parents. Standing in the doorway of David's bedroom, they look down at David, who in this version of the scene is asleep (which we're meant to assume means that he is at last sleeping peacefully).[18] However, the British censor didn't seem to realize that by substituting Kelston and Blake for David's parents, this version of the film adopts the doubles motif of the film's American version, thus unwittingly including the notion of substitution that is at the core of David's dream and which the British release changes were meant to repudiate. One of the dream's main aspects—David's desire to have parents whom he loves and trusts—has become a "reality." Perhaps most significantly, because the film's British version completely removes the sequences showing David going back to sleep and then reawakening, there is no frame story and thus no possibility that the film's preceding events could be regarded as a dream. Yet if the appearance at the film's end of Kelston and Blake are not part of a dream, what can we make of the fact that Kelston and Blake have not only replaced David's parents (who are nowhere to be seen) but repeat some of the parents' actions from the film's beginning? It would seem that despite the censor's desire for a "realistic" film with a less disturbing ending, the British version strongly suggests that David is still within a dream world.

Like many contemporary revisitings of classic films, director Tobe Hooper's 1986 remake treats the original as a joke rather than an occasion for reflection and reinterpretation. In one scene, two policemen under the Martians' control (one of whom is played by Jimmy Hunt) are searching for David in a boiler room. Hunt's character shines a light on a small glass globe that contains the Martian leader from Menzies's film.[19] Unfortunately, this joke carries no punch, and the homage accomplishes nothing except to refer us back to the film's 1953 version. Why does Hooper pull us out of the film's fiction for a weak nod to its predecessor?

Despite this drawback, the 1986 *Invaders* is very successful at showing us what it's like for a child to be afraid. Unfortunately, its conclusion is a different matter. Where Menzies's film teases us with the question of whether or not its entire scenario is a dream, judging by the remake's screenplay and the fact that in Hooper's film David never seems to go back to sleep at the end, we're encouraged to feel that the recurrence of the Martian landing is a reality. As a result, there's no sense of the equivocal or dreamlike, a loss that makes us yearn for Menzies's far more complex and rewarding film.[20]

2

HIS LITTLE TOWN: *INVASION OF THE BODY SNATCHERS*

The reason you can't go home again is not because the down-home folks are mad at you—they're not, don't flatter yourself, they couldn't care less—but because once you're in orbit and you return to Reed's drugstore on the square, you can stand no more than fifteen minutes of the conversation before you head for the woods, head for the liquor store, or head back to Martha's Vineyard, where at least you can put a tolerable and saving distance between you and home.—Walker Percy

Jack Finney's 1954 novel *The Body Snatchers* (originally serialized in *Collier's* magazine) was first adapted into a film in 1956. While the book and film's premise about aliens replacing humans is not unique, Finney did bring a special quality to his story. His book suggests a series of corollary ideas relating to dehumanization in such a way as to widen the story's significance, an attribute shared by director Don Siegel's film version.

Like the film, Finney's novel is concerned with the story of Miles Bennell, a longtime resident of and doctor in a small California town, Santa Mira. Miles regards himself as a traditionalist. In Finney's book, which is narrated by Miles, Miles states that he still makes house calls. [1] Miles also feels that the use of modern technology involves a compromise of humanistic impulses, and that it has alienated people.

Early in the book, Miles observes how progress leads to dehumanization:

> In my father's day, a night operator, whose name he'd have known, could have told him who's [just] called. It would probably have been the only light on her board at that time of night, and he'd have remembered which one it was, because they were calling the doctor. But now we have dial phones, marvelously efficient, saving you a full second or more every time you call, inhumanly perfect, and utterly brainless. [2]

The oxymoronic phrase "inhumanly perfect," which juxtaposes notions of dehumanization with technological perfection, recalls the opening narration in *Invaders from Mars*, which also links progress (in the form of advanced intelligence) with a negative quality (lack of emotion). Rather than just a Luddite embracing of the past, Miles's attitude shows that he fears progress, for certainly, there is no direct link between technological sophistication and diminished humanity. Miles's Luddism represents more than just a quaint romanticism regarding the past. It also signals a general dissatisfaction with the world. Disappointed with his small-town life, his repetitious, demanding, routine practice, and his failed marriage, Miles (at least at the book's beginning) is tired from overwork. [3] Occasionally, he compensates for his exhaustion by drinking. [4] (In fact, the book's Miles takes a drink just before his former girlfriend Becky Driscoll appears in his office.) What we see in Miles is a classic case of despair.

In *Civilization and Its Discontents*, Freud talks about how technology has not made people feel any more satisfied with their lives:

> During the last few generations mankind has made an extraordinary advance in the natural sciences and in their technical application and has established his control over nature in a way never

before imagined. . . . Men are proud of these achievements and have a right to be. But they seem to have observed that this newly-won power over space and time . . . which is the fulfillment of a longing that goes back thousands of years, has not increased the amount of pleasurable satisfaction which they may expect from life.[5]

Later in the book, Freud says that "civilized man has exchanged some part of his chances for happiness for a measure of security."[6] The problem is that in Miles's case, the freedom and security for which he longs can't be attained by journeying back into the past, nor by withdrawing into the supposedly idyllic nature of small-town life. The idealized notion of the American small town operates on the premise that one can have both homey social infrastructure and attractive career opportunities—a potentially irreconcilable combination of qualities. Moreover, the tension between the desire for freedom and the compromises to freedom that are necessary for the existence of socially cohesive towns and cities creates powerfully contradictory forces, many of which may lead to a psychosis and, especially when they are allied with a misidentification syndrome, paranoia.

In *Invasion*, the cohesiveness of small-town life yields to a horrifying form of exaggerated solidarity: a widespread lack of identity, first on the individual level and then (at least from Miles's point of view) more and more on a group level. As the result of what Miles believes to be an invasion, the town in which he and his friends Jack and Theo Belicec live is transformed into a place populated by aliens with personality characteristics with which Miles refuses to identify. Throughout the book and film, Miles is marginalized as more and more of the people in his town succumb to the invasion's effects.

Although a traditional reading of both the book and film is that Finney and Siegel are metaphorizing what was supposedly a common anxiety during the 1950s, fear of Communist infiltration, I believe that there are other things with which they are concerned. In fact, a close reading of both works shows that they contain meanings far greater than the comparatively minor ones that result if they are read politically. As an (uncredited) author on the Moria website notes about the story's film version,

> The perpetual issue that will forever dog *Invasion of the Body Snatchers* until probably film becomes obsolete is its being interpreted as an allegory about Communism and the McCarthy witch-hunts of the 1950s. It is questionable if making an anti-Communist allegory was ever Donald Siegel's intention. To call *Invasion of the Body Snatchers* a Communist allegory is perhaps to be too literal about it. Rather it seems more the case that it and others in this alien takeover genre tap into an all-pervasive state of mind. Equally as much as a parable about Communism, you could interpret *Invasion of the Body Snatchers* as a parable against conformity. Donald Siegel after all made that great parable of anti-establishment defiance *Dirty Harry* (1971).[7]

That Finney's novel is less interested in politics than in psychological and sociological observations about the effects of paranoia is clear from the many observations in the novel about what it's like to live in a small town. The book explodes the idea of small-town life's attractiveness by including a myriad of disturbing factors suggesting that Santa Mira's "placid surface"[8] masks a series of metaphors about duplication and dehumanization.

Previous to the discovery of the pods, the film's Miles had apparently regarded the town as near perfect. Yet for the book's Miles, Santa Mira is a town in which the best things that he can find to do are "hanging around the pool hall, playing solitaire, or collecting stamps."[9] A divorcé, Miles is not only socially but emotionally isolated in this quiet, uneventful little town. Miles was born and raised in Santa Mira, and has returned there to practice. Describing his residence, the book's Miles says, "I lived alone in a big old-fashioned frame house, with plenty of big trees and lots of lawn space around it. It was my parents' house before they died,"[10] a description that echoes part of what Finney says about the place where Becky lives ("a big, white, old-fashioned frame house that her father had been born in").[11] The duplication of two generations living in the same house, as well as the virtually identical wording of the passages' descriptions, suggests a lack of variety in Miles's and Becky's lives that foreshadows an alien invasion that imposes on them and their town a frightening form of sameness.

In the book and the film, Santa Mira represents certainty. For Miles and Becky, it's a familiar place. Miles and Becky left the town. Although both of them return to Santa Mira for solace (Miles finds that taking over his father's practice is convenient and comforting. Becky has come back home for emotional support after the collapse of her marriage), the fact is that what they eventually see in the town (thanks to the alien invasion bringing it into relief) is a place that suffocates them with its straitened behaviors.

Writing about the depiction of the small town in 1950s American science fiction, an author on the Moria website says,

> During this era, America saw itself as a small town. The 1950s was an era of great prosperity but was also an era of great conformity. It was the era of smalltown family values—back in the days when Family Values were universally embraced rather than conservatism's nostalgic ideals. But they were values that promulgated an impossible ideal—a middle-class lifestyle of marriage, nuclear family and *Good Housekeeping*—and refused to accept almost any variation outside of that. And outside of the smalltown state of mind there was the suspicion that there were forces gathering, things that could rampage across and destroy the small town, or more sinisterly that could take over while people weren't watching and suck out emotions. When Sloan Wilson published *The Man in the Grey Flannel Suit* (1955) it was a shock wake-up call that people felt dissatisfaction with this Utopian middle-class lifestyle that was being promoted and sold as the post-War ideal.[12]

Of course, the view that small towns foster discontent and neurosis is not unique to the 1950s. In his 1920 novel *Main Street*, Sinclair Lewis's protagonist Carol Kennicott observes,

> she saw these Scandinavian women zealously exchanging their spiced puddings and red jackets for fried pork chops and con-gealed white blouses, trading the ancient Christmas hymns of the fjords for "She's My Jazzland Cutie," being Americanized into uniformity, and in less than a generation losing in the gray-ness whatever pleasant new customs they might have added to the life of the town. Their sons finished the process. In ready-made clothes and ready-made high-school phrases they sank into propriety, and the sound American customs had absorbed without one trace of pollution another alien invasion. [13]

Carol offers a generalization about her hometown of Gopher Prairie: what goes on in it is also characteristic of other small towns. "Doubtless all small towns, in all countries, in all ages . . . have a tendency to be not only dull but mean, bitter, infested with curiosity." [14] This dullness, meanness, and bitterness, which in Fin-ney's novel are defining qualities of small-town residents, have developed out of a suppressed resentment against the atmosphere of such places. Not surprisingly, some people try to get away from this kind of environment. As Carol observes, "The more intelligent young people (and the fortunate widows!) flee to the cities with agility and, despite the fictional tradition, resolutely stay there, sel-dom returning even for holidays." [15] What they want to distance themselves from is "an unimaginatively standardized background . . . the contentment of the quiet dead, [16] who are scornful of the living for their restless walking," [17] exactly the kind of milieu from which part of Miles wants to escape, and which the pod people impose on Santa Mira, with the result that after they have trans-formed everyone in it, the town has far more uniformity than before they arrived.

Miles's anguished cry at the end of Siegel's original version of the film ("You're next!") mirrors Carol's intense concern with the spread of small-town blandness:

> A village in a country which is taking pains to become altogether standardized and pure, which aspires to succeed to Victorian England as the chief mediocrity of the world, is no longer merely provincial, no longer downy and restful in its leaf-shadowed ignorance. *It is a force seeking to dominate the earth.* [18]

Although the book's Miles seems devoted to small-town life, Santa Mira's ambience changes for him after the discovery of a body on Jack's pool table:

> The look of Throckmorton Street depressed me. It seemed littered and shabby in the morning sun, a city trash basket stood heaped and unemptied from the day before, the globe of an overhead street light was broken, and a few doors from the building where my office was, a shop stood empty. The windows were whitened, and a clumsily painted *For Rent* sign stood leaning against the glass. [19]

The previous lack of descriptive data about the town has yielded to an abundance of details, all of them negative, all the result of a shift in perception that is abrupt enough to call into question the reliability of the narrator who provides us with information. If we regard Miles clinically (as might a doctor into whose office he had walked), an interesting view of him emerges: he is dangerously unstable.

The pod people are hardly different from those in Santa Mira who haven't been changed yet. The humans are boring and uninteresting, an amorphous mass. The pod people are an undifferentiated group. *Invasion*'s aliens can be regarded as analogues of people transformed via conformity into psychological sameness, and who are now perfectly adapted to fit into a world in which many people have already been reduced to the lowest common denominator with regard to personality attributes. The pod people's only defining characteristic is a testimony to conformity run amuck: incapable of independent thought, the aliens all respond to the purely biological urge to make everyone exactly like them.

Invasion's humans say that they privilege love and other emotions, but the manner in which they express these feelings is so suppressed and routinized that they might as well not have these feelings at all. Along with Lewis's protagonist, Miles may believe that he is himself (to use Carol Kennicott's words) "being ironed into glossy mediocrity."[20] If so, his claims about the pod people's objectionability are his way of concealing from himself two truths: first, that he, too, has been changed, and second, that he has projected his own shortcomings onto those around him. And as his mania grows, more and more of those whom he had considered human succumb to a contagion whose virulence is a measure of his own psychological imbalance.

After swinging wildly between the extremes of anxiety concerning complete disruption of the prevailing social order and fantasies that attest to a desire to destroy that order, Miles finally reaps the consequences of his conflicted psychology: the placid town turns into a waking nightmare. In the book, Miles inadvertently provides a rationale for his sudden change of mood. "The human animal won't take a straight diet of emotion: fear, happiness, horror, grief, or even contentment."[21] Even after the body at Jack's is found, Miles, Becky, Jack, and Theo can still laugh and make jokes[22] but what seems to be going on is less a recovery from fear than an example of whistling in the dark.

In Finney's book, the intense effect on Miles of the transformation from small-town serenity to horror is capsulized in the description of an event that seems at first to come out of nowhere, so unprepared is the reader for the seriousness of its social commentary and the power of the emotions that are being described. This event, which is not dramatized in the film (probably because it would have been considered too inflammatory), is about an African American shoeshine man named Billy.

Miles and Becky have gone to Becky's house, where they find Becky's father, Uncle Ira, Becky's cousin Wilma, and Wilma's aunt Aleda—all of them pod people. Aleda says that she is "sorry to have missed seeing Becky." Becky's father replies, "I'm sorry, too. I thought surely she'd be home; she's back in town, you know." Uncle Ira then says, "Yes, we know, and so is Miles."[23] Previous to this dialogue, Miles had observed that the foursome "look[ed] and sound[ed] precisely the way they always had."[24] Now, after Uncle Ira's comment, Miles realizes something strange. "I wondered how they could possibly know we were back, or that we'd even been gone." At this point, Miles comments, "Then something happened, without warning, that made the hair on the back of my neck prickle and stand erect."[25]

What happens is that Miles suddenly recalls a memory about Billy. (Finney doesn't explain why this recollection occurs at this point, although the reason will soon become apparent.) In his account of the memory, Miles says, "When I was in college, a middle-aged black man had a shoeshine stand . . . and he was a town character. Everyone patronized Billy, because he was everyone's notion of what a character should be."[26] It's unclear whether Miles is aware of how ambiguous his use of the word "patronize" is. Nor does he seem to realize the paradoxical nature of his next statement. "Billy *professed* a *genuine* love for shoes."[27] Yet when Miles says that Billy "obviously took contentment in one of the simplest occupations of the world,"[28] he reveals not admiration for Billy's pleasure in doing simple things but his own patronizing appreciation for Billy's engaging in what could be regarded as a demeaning profession.

At this point, Miles recalls that very early one morning, after an evening's "student escapade," he had fallen asleep in the backseat of his car.[29] When he wakes up, he is like one of the townspeople after the invasion who are transformed while they sleep, and who awake into a world in which the human qualities of pretense and dissimulation have vanished, and in which appearances have been conquered by realities. Miles comes to understand that like many of the book's pod people, Billy despises what he does. Not only that, he also despises his customers, who unwittingly fuel his degradation. Here's Miles relating an incident between Billy and one of his friends:

> "'Morning, Bill." I couldn't see who was talking, but I heard another voice, tired and irritable, reply, "Hi, Charley," and the second voice was familiar, though I couldn't quite place it. Then it continued, in a suddenly strange and altered tone. "'Morning, Professor," it said with a queer, twisted heartiness. "'Morning!" it repeated.

Miles notes that Billy's voice was "suddenly strange and altered."[30] Soon, he says that

> the pent-up bitterness of years tainted every word and syllable [Billy] spoke. And then, for a full minute perhaps, standing there on the sidewalk of the slum he lived in, Billy went on with this quietly hysterical parody of himself. . . . Never before in my life had I heard such ugly, vicious, and bitter contempt in a voice, contempt for the people taken in by his daily antics, but even more for himself, the man who supplied the servility they bought from him.[31]

Billy then recovers his usual affable tone and the exchange ends. Nonetheless, Miles tells us that he "never again had [his] shoes shined at Billy's stand."[32] Once, though, while inadvertently passing by the shoeshine stand, Miles notices Billy's customer "smiling patronizingly" at the shoeshine man.[33] Miles says that he "turned away and walked on, ashamed for us all."[34]

Now, as abruptly as when the memory of Billy surfaced, the book once again shifts its perspective. We are back with Wilma,

Aunt Aleda, Uncle Ira, and Becky's father. Finney has Miles's memory duplicate dialogue from earlier in the book: first, Becky's father's statement from three pages earlier that "she's [Becky] back in town" and Uncle Ira's reply, "Yes, we know, and so is Miles," then some lines from much earlier in the book (page 14): Uncle Ira's questions to Miles: "How's business, Miles? Kill many to-day?"[35] Miles then comments, "For the first time in years I heard in another voice the shocking mockery I had heard in Billy's, and the short hairs of my neck actually stirred and prickled."[36] When Uncle Ira goes on to quote Miles's reply to those questions ("Bagged the limit"), Miles says that Ira's voice "parodied [his] with the pitiless sarcasm of one child taunting another."[37]

The fact that Miles has the same physical response to Billy's bitterness as he does to that of the pod foursome (the hairs on the back of his neck stand on end) connects the two events. But there is an important distinction between Billy's behavior and that of the pod people. Although Billy exhibits the same quality as the four pod people (the "parody[ing]" in Billy's case[38] echoes Uncle Ira's parodic tone),[39] Billy also exhibits a quality that the pod people do not: in Miles's word, "contempt."[40] This difference is important. Billy is able to be contemptuous because he has emotions—in this case, shame and bitterness in response to his feeling that he needs to dissimulate in order to survive. The book and film's pod people, dissimulators though they may be, have no shame about being artificial. They are capable of parody (although they never exhibit this quality in the film), but they cannot feel the distinction between what is real and what is pretense. In fact, they are incapable of feeling anything, let alone an emotional reaction such as contempt.

What Miles doesn't tell us, but what his description of Billy does, is that his former view of Billy was born of Miles's naiveté. Recall that Miles had said that Billy "obviously took contentment in one of the simpler occupations of the world."[41] But once he realizes how Billy despises his job, Miles comes to understand just how clueless he has been. The insight that Miles has as a result of hearing Billy express his true feelings signals the end of Miles's innocence, an innocence that in the book and film he tries to recover in some small way by resurrecting his old relationship with Becky, which dates back to when they were both teenagers. That this attempted resurrection of a supposedly idyllic past occurs simultaneously with Miles's discovery of what the pod people are really like suggests that the two periods in Miles's life in which these events take place share a common attribute: a lack of "the real." It's cruelly ironic that if anything, Becky's reappearance reminds the book's Miles of the time in which he could no longer believe in or experience innocence.

The pod people represent this loss of genuineness and innocence. They are powerful embodiments of pretense and prevarication, qualities that suggest innocence's opposite: corruption. In creating these beings out of what we'll soon see is his paranoia, Miles has projected onto the pod people his most profound fear: his own sense that he may not be genuine, which he then displaces onto the alien invaders. Fashioning the pod people out of his psychosis, Miles produces walking symbols of what he feels himself to be. It's not the residents of Santa Mira who (to repeat Miles's comment about Billy's tone) are "suddenly strange and altered"[42] but Miles, whose transformation was not sudden but began years back when he first discovered human hypocrisy. In the ensuing years, his anxiety about genuineness grew into a full-blown psychosis, which finally takes the form of believing that everyone is false and that only he is real.

The resurfacing of the memory about Billy, as well as the repetition of the dialogue between Becky's father and Uncle Ira, not only establishes a link in Miles's mind between Billy's hypocrisy and the pod people's artificiality. It also highlights the basis of the pod people's power. In the book and film versions of *Invasion*, the pod people are more than just duplicates that mirror certain human qualities. They are alien and alienated life forms that embody one of the most repellent human attributes: insincerity. Especially in the intensity that it takes in the pod people, this attribute makes their duplicate status that much more abhorrent.

The story about Billy makes it clear that prevaricating behavior is endemic to not only the small town of Santa Mira but society in general. If we then consider that the person telling us the story about the alien invasion is Miles (a man who in his early years was deeply repelled by insincerity), we are led to the conclusion that Miles created the pod people scenario because he feels the need to distance himself from hypocrisy, something that he believes is accomplished via a story about everyone in Santa Mira turning into an insincere double of what he feels a real human should be.

It seems likely that for the sake of social acceptability, Miles, like Billy, is hiding a series of attitudes. Miles's sexual frustration, resentment about his limited professional status, and overall dissatisfaction with his life push him toward a psychological imbalance that only needs some external event to provoke a demonstration of his true self. In Billy's case, the provocation is the subservient role that he is daily encouraged to assume. Miles's psychosis is triggered by two events: Becky's reappearance and Wilma's suspicion that her uncle is not who he appears to be.[43] Suddenly, Becky is no longer a distant memory, no longer a woman who is married and, therefore, presumably sexually inaccessible to Miles. Now, she is not only divorced but she aggressively makes it known that she is available. In the film, Becky appears in Miles's office in a strapless gown, her intentions quite clear: to resume their romance. Despite Miles's declarations to the contrary, it's apparent that her maturity and availability terrorize him, so much so that he begins to fantasize a world that is the exact opposite of the one that Becky now represents: a world of genuine emotional commitment. What Miles really wants is not the present-day Becky, a sexually experienced woman, but the virginal Becky from his high school past, with whom his most daring advance was a quick kiss on the cheek. Miles is desperately trying to recover this period, a time characterized by endearingly romantic stunts, such as when he used lipstick to put his and Becky's initials on his forehead in a sophomoric demonstration of his love for her.[44] To escape the looming reality of a relationship with a mature Becky, Miles devises a solution, which he begins to construct when Becky tells him about Wilma's worries concerning Uncle Ira. Miles starts to believe that the world is going to be taken over by beings who are not interested in love or sex—a world completely devoid of emotion, a cold, calculating place without love, desire, or physical closeness. In other words, a world that in certain respects is similar to the one in which he formerly lived, and which (despite his objections to it) he nonetheless prefers, since he regards it as essentially worry-free and safe.[45] In the book and film, the pod people are beings that embody all the qualities that Miles claims to hate. Yet when the book's Miles condemns these qualities, the person he is really criticizing is himself: a small-town doctor who lives alone, who aspires to nothing more than a limited practice, who drives a certain brand of car just to make an impression on his clientele—in short, a man whose smugness and supposedly reassuring bedside manner mask a depression and anxiety that attest to a repressed state of panic.[46]

The efforts of the film's Miles to be physically intimate with Becky are thwarted by situations having to do with the alien invaders. In the book, when Miles is kissing Becky, Jack interrupts them.[47] In the film, Miles's dinner date with Becky is interrupted by news involving aliens. Miles and Becky's embrace in his kitchen (in the midst of a domestic fantasy about the wifely Becky serving husband Miles his breakfast) is interrupted twice, first by a meter reader who may be an alien, then by Jack's coming into the room. Only once does the film's Miles kiss Becky. The event is immediately followed by her transformation into an alien. In each of these cases, we see more than a simple disturbance of events.

Like the repeated coitus interrupti in James Whale's *Bride of Frankenstein* (1935), *Invasion*'s interruptions attest to the influence of antiromantic, antisexual forces that influence the action.[48]

One of the book and film's great pleasures is that it's often unclear whether or not "people" are humans or aliens. Director Don Siegel emphasizes this indeterminacy more emphatically than Finney does. For much of the film, we are unsure at which point some of the characters have been transformed. Is Uncle Ira a pod person when we first see him? Is the town doctor Danny, who tries to convince Miles that the "body" in Becky's father's cellar is just a pile of rags, a human or an alien who has taken human form? Even more important than when the literal replacements took place is when the process of gradual transformation toward emotionless pod status began, a point that Miles's speech about humans gradually changing makes most tellingly:

> In my practice I see how people have allowed their humanity to drain away . . . only it happens slowly instead of all at once. They didn't seem to mind. . . . All of us . . . a little bit. We harden our hearts . . . grow callous . . . Only when we have to fight to stay human do we realize how precious it is to us . . . how dear . . . as you are to me.[49]

At one point in the film, Danny tries to convince Miles that being transformed into an alien leads to a very satisfying life:

> Less than a month ago, Santa Mira was like any other town. People with nothing but problems. Then out of the sky came a solution. Seeds, drifting through space for years, took root in a farmer's field. From the seeds came pods which have the power to reproduce themselves in the exact likeness of any form of life.[50]

Danny then goes on to disparage emotionality:

> Miles: You can't love or be loved, am I right?

Danny: You say it as if it were terrible. Believe me, it isn't. You've been in love before. It didn't last. It never does. [51]

Contrast this statement with Becky's assertion in the same scene that she doesn't "want a world without love or grief or beauty" [52] and it's clear that Finney and Siegel believe that to embrace life, you also need to accept life's negative qualities. Danny says that the pods represent "a solution" to the drawbacks of being human. "You're reborn into an untroubled world." [53] Miles objects that in such a world, "everyone's the same." [54] Yet a glance at the town before the pods arrive shows that Miles's implication that such sameness represents a change from what Santa Mira was already like is wrong. Santa Mira's human residents are as conformist as one could imagine. Granted, they try to make Santa Mira seem like a nice place to live. Yet its congeniality is disturbing, especially when it masks a significant amount of resentment and anxiety. [55]

The 1956 film version of Finney's novel only shows us two types of beings: the preinvasion townspeople, who appear to be agreeable, and the postinvasion, transformed townspeople, who are emotionally flat. Nowhere in the film is there the range of emotions that we encounter in the book, in which preinvasion humans harbor anger and frustration, and the postinvasion pod people have quite well-developed nastiness. By failing to place these qualities in his film, Siegel has homogenized both his humans and his pod people. As a consequence, the very aspect that Siegel wants us to find repugnant—the loss of emotions and distinctive personality attributes that result from the alien transformations—is actually prevalent in the town before the aliens begin to take over.

After the invasion, Santa Mira is essentially as it was before. When the film's Miles and Becky look at the town after it has been invaded—with people milling around the downtown square—nothing seems very different than it was at the film's beginning. The pods did not effect a change in the town. They merely brought into relief what had been happening in it all along. What the book's

Miles says of Santa Mira is also true for what the film's Miles and Becky eventually realize. "A great deal of what we saw then [dirt, decay, and vacuity: dingy hallways, shards of broken glass, flys-pecked windows, empty stores] I'd seen before, driving along Throckmorton, on my way to house calls, but I hadn't really no-ticed, hadn't really looked at this street I'd been seeing all my life."[56] He can't attribute what he sees to the townspeople's trans-formation into aliens who don't care about Santa Mira. As Miles admits, parts of the town had always been this way. It's just that the appearance of the pod people has stripped away the veneer that masked the distinction between what the town seems to be and what it really is, an effect that the aliens have on the town's resi-dents as well. The thin barrier between apparent normalcy and real alienation has disappeared. "Miles, when did this *happen?*" the book's Becky asks about the town's transformation from idyllicism to ugly reality, to which Miles replies, "A little at a time."[57] The parallel between this exchange and Miles's statement in the film that people lose their humanity by small but progressive degrees[58] indicates that, at least in this respect, screenwriter Daniel Mainwar-ing has carried over intact one of the book's most telling elements: its critique of a dehumanization caused not by alien takeover but by people's indifference to the quality of their lives.

Now, I want to consider the book and film as texts that exemplify certain aspects of clinical psychopathology. Consider first the situa-tion in the film: Doesn't it strain even fictional plausibility that an entire town has been taken over by aliens, that only one man has survived as a human, and that this human happens to be the person telling the story? Miles's conviction that the people in Santa Mira are being replaced by aliens sounds like the tale of a classic para-noiac.

Psychologists Daniel Freeman and Philippa Garety note that "a belief may persist as a result of two processes: obtaining confirmatory evidence, or discarding disconfirmatory evidence."[59] Miles exhibits both of these behaviors. In the film, Miles initially accepts Jack's contention that the body on his pool table is not human. Then, after Danny emphatically states that it is a human body, Miles agrees with this point of view, although he quickly returns to his original belief when he sees what he believes is a duplicate Becky in her father's basement. Miles then relinquishes this notion after Danny convinces him that what he saw in Becky's basement was the result of a delusion. At this point in the film, Miles continually swings between polarized ideas about the infestation that is supposedly sweeping the town. Yet only a little while later, Miles passes from doubt to a frighteningly uninformed certitude.

By the time that he has finally convinced himself that the invasion scenario is valid, Miles is firmly rooted in a deep psychosis characterized by a classic paranoia symptom known as "confirmation bias." Freeman and Garety note,

> The confirmation bias is a normal tendency to look for evidence consistent with beliefs, but not for evidence that is inconsistent with beliefs . . . evidence supportive of persecutory beliefs will be accumulated. . . . There is evidence that individuals with persecutory delusions attribute the cause of negative events to other people rather than themselves or situations. Thus, authentication of the delusion will occur; for example, the cause of headaches may be attributed to a malevolent power. . . .
>
> In contrast, theories have not addressed how disconfirmatory evidence is discarded. Only Melges and Freeman (1975, p. 1041) make passing reference to this issue when they set out their cybernetic model of persecutory delusions:
>
> > The ruminative vicious cycle common to this stage can be paraphrased as follows: "If I do this, they will do that; and if they don't do that, it's because they are pretending (much like I am) in order to catch me off guard later on." In this way, his predictions are confirmed no matter what happens, and his seemingly correct predictions ensnare him further

in what seems to be a preordained web of events determined by others.

In other words, disconfirmatory evidence is dismissed because individuals view it as instances of the deviousness of the
persecutors.[60]

Alternating between diametrically opposite explanations for
what he perceives as the strange goings-on in Santa Mira, Miles
settles on the theory that all of it can be explained by an alien
invasion scenario. Once Miles accepts this scenario's validity,
everything begins to make sense to him because he has adopted a
point of view that orders what formerly seemed to be a random
series of unusual events. Miles is so committed to this delusion that
its improbability (and the possibility that it is he, and not the town,
that has been taken over) never occurs to him. To Miles, all
contrary opinions seem ill-founded. To say that a person with
Miles's condition is devoted to an alternate weltanschauung is in-
sufficient. Such a person has embraced a new belief system so
completely that it has displaced not only differing viewpoints but
even the notion that such viewpoints exist.

Viewing Miles as a paranoiac makes possible an additional explanation for his obsessive thinking. The psychological condition
known as Capgras' syndrome is defined by psychiatrists M. David
Enoch and Hadrian Ball as "an uncommon, colourful syndrome in
which the patient believes that a person, usually closely related to
him, has been replaced by an exact double." This "delusion of
doubles" is considered to be a "chronic paranoid psychosis."[61]
Enoch and Ball point out that "Capgras' syndrome is the best
known and most frequently occurring example of the delusional
misidentification syndromes."[62] Interestingly, in the traditional
view of Capgras (which to a degree has been supplanted by an
organic explanation for the condition's development), the syndrome is also often associated with the same kind of psychological

experience that Miles is undergoing: depersonalization, a term that has multiple meanings in *Invasion*, in which people lose their identities.[63]

For the person with Capgras, affinity is transformed into distance: those who are familiar become the Other, the unknown. Enoch and Ball state that "it is significant how often the patients themselves use the words 'doubles' and 'impostors' to describe the misidentified person. One patient categorically affirmed 'She is her double.'"[64] The psychodynamics of this syndrome are more complex than this explanation suggests, though. "Capgras' phenomenon, when reduced down to its essence, is basically a love-hate conflict that is resolved by projecting ambivalent feelings onto an imaginary double."[65] Toward whom does Miles feel this ambivalence? Becky, to whom he is attracted and by whom he is repelled. Miles notices Becky's desire for a renewal of their relationship, which causes Miles severe anxiety. He represses this anxiety, masking it with what he believes is an interest in her. Finally, Miles begins to view Becky as an alien, and the Becky problem is solved.

Enoch and Ball go on to say, "In those cases where it occurs it is very significant that before the onset of the delusion of doubles the patient exhibits increased affection and sexual craving towards the object. This excessive reaction results from a craving for reassurance regarding the loss of the object and the simultaneous fear of losing it."[66] In the book and film, we see this reaction in Miles's repeated attempts to seduce Becky.

The conclusion of Siegel's version of the story is suitably depressing. Miles is last seen on the town's periphery, in the middle of a highway, shouting at passing motorists.[67] Judging from the physical location, one might think that his flight from the town had also taken him to the border of his delusion, from which he is about to be freed. Instead, once Miles is on the highway, he encounters another example of his delusion: a truckload of what appear to be seed pods. At *Invasion*'s end, paranoia, which has taken root in and been nurtured by the small town's claustrophobic feel and its residents' insufferable conformism, germinates and spreads beyond its confines, threatening to take over any part of the world that Miles is capable of imagining. For Miles, the heavens and Earth are filled with madness. Hell's doors haven't just opened. They've been ripped from their hinges.

3

ECCE HUMANITAS: *THE DAY THE EARTH STOOD STILL*

If atomic bombs are to be added as new weapons to the arsenals of a warring world, or to the arsenals of the nations preparing for war, then the time will come when mankind will curse the names of Los Alamos and Hiroshima. The people of this world must unite or they will perish.—J. Robert Oppenheimer

Didactic without being strident, ethical without being preachy, director Robert Wise's *The Day the Earth Stood Still* (1951) accomplishes everything that the other films in this book do but more gracefully and intelligently. *Day*'s invasion is not a penetration into the dream realm nor an incursion against the institutions of marriage or the home. Instead, it's an attempt to influence humans' attitude toward military use of atomic power, whose potential for cataclysm the film views as an example of the human capacity for self-destruction. That the film promoted responsible use of nuclear power and also took a pacifist political stance during a decade in which such attitudes were not particularly popular is a testament to its integrity. As critic M. Keith Booker notes,

> Despite its highly influential look and sound, *The Day the Earth Stood Still* is probably best remembered today not for its technical accomplishments but for its advocacy of peace and interna-

tional cooperation, an advocacy made all the more striking by
the fact that the film appeared during the Korean War and thus
at the very height of international Cold War tensions. [1]

The Day the Earth Stood Still was adapted by scriptwriter Edmund North from Harry Bates's 1940 short story "Farewell to the
Master." [2] Bates's story is notable for two things. First, it contains
the suggestion that the alien Klaatu, who is twice described as
"godlike in appearance and human in form," is capable of being
resurrected. More importantly, the story tells us that of the two
aliens who come to Earth, it is not Klaatu but the robot Gort who is
the master. This idea is transformed in the film into the notion that
just as Klaatu's people needed an all-powerful force to stop them
from destroying themselves so, too, do humans.

The film's Klaatu arrives on Earth clad in a glistening silver
spacesuit with a helmet. Once he removes the helmet, Klaatu (Michael Rennie) looks human. What's more, he has neither strange
powers nor a menacing attitude. This alien seems restrained, reasonable, and ethical. He's not xenophobic (as is the film's Mrs.
Barley) nor jingoistic, jealous, or sexist, as is Tom (Hugh Marlowe), the boyfriend of Patricia Neal's Helen Benson.

Although we're meant to see Klaatu as a model of high intelligence and sophisticated thinking, it's clear that his common sense
is not that well developed. Not only that, but he sometimes seems
somewhat foolish. Why does he find it so difficult to understand
humans' tendency to become embroiled in pointless rivalries, as
well as their inability to govern their destructive behavior in the
absence of an external threat, when the people of his own planet
were similarly contentious and inept? Moreover, why do Klaatu
and his people believe that it's a good idea to bring their proposal
that humans abjure military use of nuclear weapons to scientists,
the group that helped to develop these weapons? And yet, ironically, the only group in the film that appears to be concerned with
peace are scientists, many of whom gather at the site of Klaatu's

parting speech. Nonetheless, the only character in the film that draws attention to atomic weapons' threat to human survival is Klaatu, even though his primary concern is not for humans but for his own people. As Klaatu says at the film's end, his civilization doesn't care what Earthlings do as long as they don't threaten the safety of other planets.

To use wording from one of the film's posters, Klaatu comes to Earth with "a warning and an ultimatum": either humans repress their aggressive development of advanced weaponry (a tendency that Klaatu believes will result in their use of atomic bombs in outer space) or their planet will be destroyed. In an early scene, Klaatu proposes the idealistic notion that all of the world's leaders be brought together so that he can tell them the purpose of his visit. The American president's representative, Mr. Harley (Frank Conroy), points out the problem with this idea:

HARLEY
(shocked and perturbed by [Klaatu's] notion)
I'm afraid that would be a little awkward. It's—it's completely without precedent. And there are practical considerations—the time involved—the enormous distances.[3]

Eventually, Harley gives Klaatu the real reason for why he believes that Klaatu's idea is impractical. "Believe me, you don't understand. [The heads of state] wouldn't sit down at the same table."[4]

In response, Klaatu refers to humans' "childish jealousies and suspicions,"[5] the implication being that he and his people have evolved beyond such attitudes. For Klaatu, Earthlings' focus on their own desires to the exclusion of others' needs is representative of their pettiness. He comes to recognize that humans operate on the basis of a pathological form of the Freudian pleasure principle, and are therefore unable to privilege not only higher impulses such as concern for others but even self-serving interests such as self-preservation.

In the chapter "Ecce Homo" of his book *On Aggression*, Konrad Lorenz writes,

> Let us imagine that an absolutely unbiased investigator on another planet, perhaps Mars, is examining human behavior on Earth, with the aid of a telescope whose magnification is too small to enable him to discern individuals and follow their separate behavior, or large enough for him to observe occurrences such as migrations of peoples, wars, and similar great historical events. He would never gain the impression that human behavior was dictated by intelligence, still less by responsible morality.[6]

This is the viewpoint on which Klaatu bases his judgment of humans. He has no intimate knowledge of individual human behavior, which is why he decides to venture out incognito among Washington's citizens. Unfortunately, even after he has spent time with various people, Klaatu still can't understand humans' tendency to be unreasonable. He finally decides that the only way to change human behavior is by threatening them.

Lorenz would tend to agree with Klaatu's decision. "In reality, even the fullest rational insight into the consequences of an action and into the logical consistency of its premise would not result in an imperative or in a prohibition, were it not for some emotional, in other words instinctive, source of energy supplying motivation."[7] What quality in human beings should be operating in order to prevent the types of intraspecies aggression that Klaatu feels is a danger to the rest of the galaxy? Lorenz refers to this faculty as "rational responsibility," a term that he expands when he refers to "rational, responsible morality":[8]

> As I have already explained in [this book's] chapter on behavior mechanisms functionally analogous to morality, all heavily armed carnivores possess sufficiently reliable inhibitions which

prevent the self-destruction of the species. [However], no selec-
tion pressure arose in the prehistory of mankind to breed inhibitory mechanisms preventing the killing of conspecifics until, all
of a sudden, the invention of artificial weapons upset the equilibrium of killing potential and social inhibitions. When it did,
man's position was very nearly that of a dove which, by some
unnatural trick of nature, suddenly acquired the beak of a ra-
ven.[9]

However, these assertions rest on faulty premises. Even conventional arms give humans the capability to destroy large numbers of
their own species. The introduction of advanced weaponry merely
increased the scale at which humans could be killed.

Unfortunately, an inhibitory mechanism often does not come
into play in large-scale modern-day warfare because some of it is
either automated, involves the use of extremely destructive technology, or occurs at what Lorenz refers to as a "distance."[10] Lorenz
writes that "the deep, emotional layers of your personality simply
do not register the fact that the crooking of the forefinger to release
a shot tears the entrails of another man."[11] It seems obvious that it's
precisely because of "distance" that humans don't really care how
their actions may affect residents of other planets. What can't under
any circumstances be understood, though, is why they don't even
seem to care what happens to themselves and their own planet.[12]

If an appeal to humans' reasonableness is doomed to fail, on
what mechanism can Klaatu rely to ensure his mission's success?
Aside from frightening people into disarming, perhaps an emotional approach would be productive—hence Klaatu's developing a
close relationship with Helen. Unlike most of the film's characters,
Helen appreciates the importance of Klaatu's warnings. At least for
a time, she protects him from the military and repudiates the representative of humans' major shortcomings (Tom), whose actions
place Klaatu in danger.

The initial contact between Klaatu and humans exemplifies the
former's ignorance and the latter's suspicious attitudes. Klaatu's

offering of an interplanetary communications device is taken by a soldier as a sign of aggression. To a certain extent, the soldier's response is understandable. Klaatu draws the device from his garment in such a way as to (inadvertently) make it seem as though he is removing it from a holster. Klaatu points the device forward and then engages it, which causes metallic extensions to shoot out. The suddenness of this last movement exacerbates the already-high level of tension among the military. A soldier shoots Klaatu in the shoulder. Even after the arrival of a superior officer, who casts a disparaging look at the soldier who fired the shot, this tension is not dissipated. When Klaatu tries to stand up, two of the soldiers standing near him, in what is clearly a reflex action, reach for their guns.

Commenting on this scene and how emblematic its action is of the majority of human reactions to which Klaatu is subjected throughout the film, *Day*'s producer, Julian Blaustein, says,

> The thing that grabbed my attention was the response of people to the unknown. Klaatu holds his hand up with something that looks unfamiliar to them and he is immediately shot. It was a terribly significant moment for me in terms of story. It really started the whole thing going. [13]

The scene accomplishes two important things: it foreshadows the scene toward the film's end in which Klaatu is once again shot by a soldier and exemplifies Klaatu's trust in people (even though his previous knowledge of human behavior should have told him how prone to overreaction many humans are). [14]

After going with Helen's son Bobby to Arlington Cemetery, Klaatu and the boy visit the Lincoln Memorial. Klaatu's respect for the intelligence behind the Gettysburg Address leads him to a thought: if he cannot speak to all of the world's political leaders, then perhaps he should contact the "smartest man in America," a man regarded as one of the world's top scientists: Professor Barnhardt (Sam Jaffee).

Despite the attractive, quirky attributes that the filmmakers give him (a studied manner of speaking, an Einsteinian hairdo), Barnhardt may not be the wisest choice for the man to whom Klaatu reveals his true identity. For one thing, the math problem that Klaatu sees on Barnhardt's blackboard involves celestial mechanics. A subfield in this discipline deals not only with the actions of orbital satellites but the use of rockets. It's likely that the solution to the problem that Barnhardt is working on would result in the production of rockets armed with atomic warheads, precisely the type of technology that prompted Klaatu's visit to Earth. This speculation about Barnhardt's work is confirmed by the film's screenplay. In a scene from North's script that doesn't appear in the film, Klaatu is detained at a police station. During the scene, Klaatu is asked why he was at Barnhardt's house. The lieutenant questioning Klaatu says, "I suppose you know that Barnhardt does a lot of secret work for the Army."[15] Later, Klaatu tells the professor that his people developed their aversion to the use of atomic weapons after a series of wars in which atom bombs were used.[16] And yet, astoundingly, the film shows us Klaatu helping Barnhardt design a destructive technology that's being sent into outer space, where it can threaten the safety of interplanetary civilizations. Since Klaatu knows that humans lack the restraint to avoid using weapons for destructive purposes, it's difficult to understand his behavior.

Although *Day* would have us believe that scientists are intelligent and responsible individuals who conscientiously wield technology, this view is not supported by the film's action. Barnhardt seems to take a childish delight in seeing Klaatu's technical capability stop most of the planet's electric motors. Of course, one could argue that what pleases Barnhardt about people's fearful responses to Klaatu's experiment is his anticipation of the ultimate effect of these reactions: the development of appreciation for the necessity of using technology with restraint. The fact is, though, that neither Barnhardt nor Klaatu intends for people to have such a reasonable reaction nor to process their fear in this way. Instead, what they both hope for is to terrify people into changing their behavior.

Implicitly, *Day* references the scientists who worked on the Manhattan Project, who were called upon to develop a form of power that from the outset they knew would be used for a military purpose. On the one hand, these researchers' intellectual curiosity drove them forward. Like Colonel Nicholson in David Lean's 1957 film *The Bridge on the River Kwai*, they were confronted with a massive technical challenge and rose to it, sometimes losing sight of how their project was to be used. At other times, though, these scientists' ethics not only called into question the morality of their actions but the manner in which the results of their efforts might be applied.

Writing about his and his colleagues' work on the project, Robert Oppenheimer says,

> Despite the vision and farseeing wisdom of our wartime heads of state, the physicists have felt the peculiarly intimate responsibility for suggesting, for supporting, and in the end, in large measure, for achieving the realization of atomic weapons. Nor can we forget that these weapons as they were in fact used dramatized so mercilessly the inhumanity and evil of modern war. In some sort of crude sense which no vulgarity, no humor, no overstatement can quite extinguish, the physicists have known sin; and this is a knowledge which they cannot lose. [17]

Oppenheimer made plain the nature of this sin in his oft-quoted remark about the Manhattan Project's atom bomb test explosion:

> We knew the world would not be the same. A few people laughed, a few people cried, most people were silent. I remembered the line from the Hindu scripture, the Bhagavad-Gita. . . . "Now, I am become Death, the destroyer of worlds." I suppose we all thought that, one way or another. [18]

Yet despite all of his ex post facto moralizing, Oppenheimer never repudiated an essential aspect of his attitude toward science: that it involves indulging a desire for knowledge that often, especially at the investigative stage, disregards how that knowledge may be used. Oppenheimer once said,

> When you see something that is technically sweet, you go ahead and do it and argue about what to do about it only after you've had your technical success. That is the way it was with the atomic bomb.[19]

Here we have the essential dilemma in the film. As a civilization advances so, too, does its technology. The technology may be as complex as atomic weaponry or as simple as fire. The central question still remains: How will this technology be used, and what will be the consequences of these uses? Virtually every technology has the capability to be both productive and destructive. What's of primary importance is whether people's ability to make rational judgments comes into play when the use of this technology is considered.

The notion of rationality is prominent during the scene in which Klaatu and Bobby are at the ship's landing site.[20] At the end of a radio reporter's interview with a woman, the reporter says, "Thank you, Mrs. Robinson. I'm sure we've all shared your fears these past few days." When he reaches Klaatu, the reporter solicits his response to the alien landing. Klaatu says that it is not acceptable to substitute "fear for reason," at which point the reporter cuts him off.[21] Although Wise's point in this scene is directed at the anti-Communism that was prevalent in the United States at the time, the critique is more far reaching than that. Most people's reactions to Klaatu's visit are xenophobic. Rooming house tenant Mrs. Barley (Frances Bavier), who's reading a newspaper with a two-page drawing of a menacing robot and panic-stricken people that features the headline "Are We Long for This World?"[22] implies that the aliens whom she is certain have come to Earth for conquest are not really aliens at all but humans (as she says, from "you know where . . .").[23] In fact, if you consider the behavior of virtually all of the film's characters, you get the impression that *Day* highlights humans' negative qualities, in particular their paranoiac self-destructiveness and aggression. It could be said that Klaatu and Helen embody ideals that humans could emulate. Yet the effect that most of the other characters have on us tends to overwhelm the values that this duo embodies. Often, the film makes it seem as though the planet is not worth saving.

Klaatu does not represent an alternative to this unfortunate situation. Along with his gentle demeanor and his compassion, he is also retributive. Klaatu would argue that his threat to destroy the Earth if humans do not repudiate militarism represents his people's effort to protect themselves. "But soon you will apply atomic energy to spaceships—and then you become a threat to the peace and security of other planets. That, of course, we cannot tolerate," Klaatu says.[24] Yet surely there are alternatives to Klaatu's preemptive plan. Since Klaatu can render Earth's electricity useless, he probably could also neutralize all of its atomic weapons and the rockets that would propel them into space. However, such a solution would not address the underlying problem with regard to such weaponry: humans' pleasure in aggression, a tendency that as yet no one has been completely able to restrain.

For Klaatu, as for the American seventeenth-century minister Jonathan Edwards, there is no middle ground between damnation and redemption. Klaatu presents humans with Manichean alternatives: live or die. Edwards presents his congregation with a comparable choice:

> O sinner! Consider the fearful danger you are in: it is a great furnace of wrath, a wide and bottomless pit, full of the fire of wrath, that you are held over in the hand of that God, whose wrath is provoked and incensed as much against you, as against

many of the damned in hell. You hang by a slender thread, with the flames of divine wrath flashing about it, and ready every moment to singe it, and burn it asunder.[25]

The purpose in both cases is clear: in Edwards's words, "awakening unconverted persons."[26]

To a degree, *Day* tempers Edwards's fire-and-brimstone approach with touches of humanism in order to make the film's message more palatable to a general audience. Ultimately, though, beneath the humanism that North has given Klaatu in order to make what he says less off-putting there is still an unyielding fundamentalism, as is quite evident in Klaatu's final speech:

> The Universe grows smaller every day and the threat of aggression by any group—anywhere—can no longer be tolerated. There must be security for all or no one is secure. . . . This does not mean giving up any freedom except the freedom to act irresponsibly. . . . I came here to give you the facts. It is no concern of ours how you run your own planet—but if you threaten to extend your violence, this Earth of yours will be reduced to a burned-out cinder. Your choice is simple. Join us and live in peace. Or pursue your present course—and face obliteration. We will be waiting for your answer. The decision rests with you.[27]

Klaatu and Edwards believe that achieving redemption requires both volition and divine intervention in the form of grace. In *Day*, the type of grace being proposed is prevenient grace:

> Orthodox theology teaches prevenient grace, meaning that God makes the first movement toward man, and that salvation is impossible from our own will alone. However, man is endowed with free will, and an individual can either accept or reject the grace of God. Thus an individual must cooperate with God's grace to be saved, though he can claim no credit of his own, as any progress he makes is possible only by the grace of God.[28]

Like God, Klaatu gives humans a final chance to redeem them-selves and be spared destruction. Ultimately, though, the wrath that is promised should the wrong choice be made is harsher than God's because not even the planet will be spared. In essence, Klaatu will call down upon Earth the same destructive fury of which Isaiah speaks in a passage quoted by Edwards in his sermon. *"For behold, the Lord will come with fire, and with his chariots like a whirlwind, to render his anger with fury, and his rebuke with flames of fire."*[29] In *The Day the Earth Stood Still,* the invasion can have a good outcome but only if humans completely reform their behavior.

The Day the Earth Still states its case for rational restraint in a compelling way. Everyone with an interest in sci-fi loves this film. It represents a heartfelt plea that humans resist aggression in all forms. Make no mistake, though. The film leaves humans only one choice if they want to survive. And frankly, that's all they really need.[30]

4

WE DON'T LIKE YOUR KIND HERE: *IT CAME FROM OUTER SPACE*

There is nothing more frightful than ignorance in action.
—Johann Wolfgang von Goethe

Although the notion of the "Other" is present in many 1950s American sci-fi films, in no other film of this period is it dealt with as blatantly, and with such conviction, as in director Jack Arnold's *It Came from Outer Space* (1953). Via the use of metaphor, the film suggests that the standard view of 1950s science fiction films—that American society is rife with phobias concerning trends that are beyond an individual's control (e.g., the proliferation of atomic weapons, the threat of nuclear war, the supposed spread of Communism in the United States)—is incorrect. *It Came* does contend that Americans have real fears. However, in the film's view, those fears are self-created: in particular, the xenophobia that to a significant extent results from small-town insularity. The townspeople in the film are repeatedly shown to be petty in their treatment of "Others." If we extrapolate from the film and generalize its situations, we're led to the conclusion that many Americans in the 1950s were afraid of atomic power and Communism not because they were real threats but because they had yielded to a neurotic point of view within which threats are seen everywhere. The solution to such a pathology is suggested in *It Came*: people need to develop understanding and compassion for each other.

It Came inverts one of the usual paradigms in 1950s sci-fi films: the notion that invaders maliciously intend to conquer the world. The film's aliens want no part of life on Earth. Unlike the intergalactic visitors in films such as *The Thing from Another World, Kronos,* or *The War of the Worlds,* in *It Came*, it is not the humans but the aliens who are alienated. The film's otherworldly visitors are shy, introverted, reclusive, and peaceful. They don't take over people's minds, as they do in *Invaders from Mars*. And while *It Came*'s aliens do create duplicates, they only do so in order to effect as quick a departure from Earth as possible.

If anything, these creatures have personal characteristics that Americans attributed to themselves in the 1950s: they're peace loving and cooperative. By contrast, the majority of the film's Americans are jealous, defensive, rageful, and prone to violence. Some of the film's humans form themselves into a mob that threatens the aliens with destruction. This mob actually murders one of the aliens—not because the aliens are a threat, but because they are perceived as being different. Because the aliens have landed near their town, the citizens of Sand Rock, Arizona, become distressed, which suggests that on a very deep emotional level, the film is not about intergalactic monsters but the monsters that humans become when they act on their anxieties about people who are different from them in some way. In this sense, *It Came* is a metaphoric film about race relations, in the same manner as is Philip Dick's novel *Do Androids Dream of Electric Sheep?*, which was the basis for director Ridley Scott's film *Blade Runner* (1982).

There are similarities between *It Came*'s aliens and those in other 1950s science fiction films, in particular the absence of emotion, but this quality can be explained two ways: either as the result of the aliens' faulty duplication process or as a cautionary gesture that they adopt. The latter attitude mirrors a type of behavior used by some immigrants or minorities who, to protect themselves against aggression, make themselves "invisible" by minimizing vocalizations, actions, and gestures that would distinguish them, and by dressing as conventionally as possible in order to blend in. (Ralph Ellison makes this precise point in his novel *Invisible Man*.)

The film's aliens have a counterpart in a human: amateur astronomer John Putnam (Richard Carlson). While the film's invocation of the scientist reluctant to marry his girlfriend is familiar (we will see it again in *Kronos*), what is not usual is the degree to which John is marginalized in his community. Among the reasons for John's marginalization is his insistence that he live on his own terms. John defies conventionality by remaining alone with his girlfriend until late at night, thereby risking gossip from the townspeople. On a professional level, John is also something of a rogue. Like *Invaders from Mars*' David, he accepts the possibility of intergalactic life. This attitude brings with it the notion that alternative civilizations may have values different from those of humans, with the consequence that one cannot then be certain that human forms of behavior are the right way to live. As a result, John is quite unlike his fellow townsfolk, whom he describes as being confident about themselves and their place in the universe. In a way, John is the first alien we meet in the film.

John's girlfriend, Ellen Fields (Barbara Rush), is midway between John and the town's values. She stays with John until late in the evening, is absent from her job after the aliens land, and, as we will see, cannot shake herself loose from some fairly traditional values. In his desire for the town to believe that he has sighted a ship, John also affirms a need that he says he does not have: the desire, if not to be accepted by the townspeople, at least to have his word believed by them. In this respect, John is again like *Invaders*' David (and *Invasion of the Body Snatchers*' Miles): he wants people whom he doesn't respect to trust that what he says is the truth. In this regard, John is also like some newly-arrived immigrants who feel alienated from a culture that they nonetheless want to join. John wants, and doesn't want, to be part of a group that would have him as a member.

John's marginalization, which is to a significant degree self-imposed, is made plain at the film's beginning. His house is on the outskirts of town, in the desert. Such a location is certainly useful in that it is free from the light pollution associated with cities, which would compromise his view of the stars. For John, though, the major pollution that occurs in cities is the kind that arises from people's narrow opinions about what is and is not real and possible, which thereby obscures their ability to see and accept things that don't conform to their idea of reality. What John seeks by distancing himself from this metaphoric pollution is a clear, unprejudiced view of the universe's possibilities, regardless of the forms that these possibilities may take. Unable to find satisfaction among the town's humans, John seeks solace in two areas: in a relationship with his girlfriend that is built on isolation, and in an intellectual relation with the cosmos that is premised on an unobstructed view of what exists, regardless of preconceptions.

Adding to John's alienation is the event that begins the film's action. John sees something, the nature of which even Ellen doubts: an intergalactic object that plunges to the Earth and crashes. The first quarter of the film concerns itself with the townspeople (and, for a while, Ellen) disbelieving John's assertion that what he has seen is not a meteor but a spacecraft. The alienated role into which John is cast is partially a result of his own self-righteous attitude and part the result of the townspeople's intolerance. Though there's no way to separate the contributing factors in this situation, it is clear that, as we'll see, in many ways the film appropriates classic conceits from American westerns. In the film, John is a lone rider in pursuit of truth, a man who sees himself as the sole opposition to the racist, jingoist tendencies of the town on whose literal and symbolic fringes he lives.

John's desert house offers him a refuge from what he regards as the critical attitude that the townspeople have toward him. "They've talked about me before," he tells Ellen. Unable to rely on other human beings for emotional and psychological support, John takes refuge in a hermit-like life, within which he gazes at the stars, which provide him not only with distraction but an appreciation of beauty unsullied by human commerce. It's therefore somewhat ironic that after what only appears to be a comet crash, what he finds in the desert is a group of beings just as isolated and misunderstood as he is, and whom the townspeople subject to a hostility based on ignorance. That the alienated human is the first to contact the aliens tells us less about the film's use of irony than about the way that, as in other films, abstract concepts are expressed through concrete representations. In *It Came*, the central concept that is metaphorized is xenophobia.

John's opening voiceover narration says of Sand Rock that "it's a nice town, knowing its past and sure of its future, as it makes ready for the night, and the predictable morning." However, the first assertion is belied by John's wanting to live outside of town, the second speaks more to the town's ignorance (or arrogance) than to its sense of self-assurance, while the third is soon to be contradicted by the arrival of the aliens. In an unconscious attempt to connect himself to the town, John then says that in his house, "we're also sure of the future, so very sure," although what he is referring to is not economic or social progress but romantic love's developing into marriage. When we first see John and Ellen, it's just after dinner. Both of them are sitting before the fire. Ellen stands over John, apparently lost in thought. John sits staring into the fire, musing. When they leave the house to look through John's telescope, they begin a short discussion about how suitable they are for each other. Ellen's contention is that astrologically, they are quite compatible. The reference to astronomical influences not only anticipates the arrival of the meteor and the subsequent effect that the presence of the aliens will have on their lives but also hints at the notion that humans do not have complete control over their destinies. If Ellen and John were meant to meet, the same could be said of John and the aliens. And if, as we'll see in later scenes, the aliens begin to distrust John—after which Ellen's alien double attempts to kill him—what we may be seeing is a playing out of John's worst fears concerning his girlfriend: that her supposedly romantic interest in marriage masks her desire to metaphorically murder the type of person he currently is.

Even if we accept the dinner scene at face value, there is still another disturbing element. Just as John and Ellen are about to embrace, the alien ship (looking like a meteor) streaks across the sky and crashes in the distance. The symbolic coitus interruptus suggests that what the aliens represent is the antithesis of consummated passion. Since the film's aliens are embodiments of classic alienation, and since the most alienated characters in the film are townspeople, we're encouraged to conclude that the town has a vested interest in preventing the consummation of John and Ellen's love, a premise that is repeatedly demonstrated through *It Came*'s action.

The after-dinner adjournment to the telescope is auspicious in one sense, though: it places John and Ellen at the exact spot where they can have an unobstructed view of the alien ship in flight. Naturally curious, John goes to investigate the crash site. What he finds is a spherical object half-buried in the side of a mountain. After descending into the crater created by the ship's impact, John comes face-to-face with the craft's outside, within which there is an open portal, through which John can barely discern a being whose shape is not human. Not wishing to be investigated, the aliens cause a rockslide, which buries their ship.

The level of anxiety that the film's opening anomalous events creates begins to pollute situations that under "normal" circumstances would seem mundane. Out in the desert, Ellen mistakes part of a Joshua tree for an alien's eyes. A bit later in film, even though she has accepted John's view of the aliens as harmless, she is startled to the point of screaming by a young boy who comes to the front door of John's home wearing what is obviously a plastic toy space helmet (which clearly says "space helmet" on it). Even John is affected by the aliens' presence on the outskirts of town. In one scene, he enters the mine in which the aliens are located carrying two objects that reflect the duality of his attitude: a gun, which signals his willingness to do violence (in which respect he is like the townspeople) and a flashlight, whose link to his telescope as a device that aids discovery signals his desire to learn the true significance of the aliens' presence.

Contrary to what we might expect, the film's resident scientist is unwilling to believe John's contention that the "meteor" was really a spacecraft. Dr. Snell (George Eldredge) tries to convince John that what he believes he has seen is nothing more than the result of an overwrought imagination. Snell points out to John the lack of residual radiation near the crash site (which one would expect had an intergalactic craft crashed there), and what appears to Snell to be a fusing of rocks typical of a meteor crash. Yet Snell only sees what his expectations allow him to see. In dismay, John replies, "I don't know what's odd and what isn't anymore. But I do know that I expected you to be more open to the idea than the others. You're a man of science." Snell's response is exaggerated and unjustified. "And therefore less inclined to witchcraft," he says. But where in the observations that John relates has there been any hint at the existence of something occult? If anything, the situation in the current scene is just the reverse. John is adopting an empirical attitude toward his experience. If any demonizing is going on, it's Snell who's doing it when he unjustifiably criticizes John.

John's response to Snell's comment is impassioned. "Not witchcraft, Dr. Snell, imagination. Willingness to believe that there are lots of things that we don't know anything about." John goes on to detail some previous conventional notions that were subsequently proved to be factually incorrect, such as the belief that the Earth was a "level plane" and that the stars were "lamps held from the sky." By making these comparisons, John is implying that Snell's mode of thinking is outmoded. More significantly, though, John is drawing attention to the kind of narrow-minded thought process that not only makes possible but justifies traditional views of not just reality but the kinds of life forms that are "acceptable" within that reality. The type of science that Snell practices is no more than an academically tinged version of the bigotry that the town's residents exhibit against the alien visitors, whose thinking, behavior, or appearance differ from a predetermined norm, and who thereby threaten the fragile beliefs of people who neurotically cling to atavistic ideas. All that Snell can offer is acceptance of the traditional paradigm of perception, of things as they are (and, for him, as they always will be). "Be realistic, John," Snell says, thereby overlooking the fact that what science regards as real is constantly subject to change.[1]

Snell isn't suggesting that John conform to the situation's facts, because that is precisely what John is doing. Rather, he's telling John to be practical, to accept the conventional view of reality for the sake of avoiding social marginalization. But why would someone repudiate a point of view that one believes in just for the sake of being part of the majority? Essentially, Snell is suggesting that John join the same type of unthinking crowd that later in the film becomes an angry, homicidal mob. We've seen an example of this type of mob before: the mass of townspeople that pursues Miles and Becky in *Invasion of the Body Snatchers*.

What Snell lacks is not only a vision of the future but a necessary component for any scientist: curiosity. He embodies a rigid, categorical worldview that in effect is no different than that of the town's sheriff, Matt Warren (Charles Drake), who operates in response to the most unconsidered, basic impulses: love, jealousy, envy, hate. Like the writers whom Victor Frankenstein's father warned him not to read (Paracelsus, Albertus Magnus), John is offering an alternate view of the cosmos, and is experiencing the same type of response from people that these writers encountered: rage, disbelief, ridicule. In place of imagination, Snell offers conventional reality. Snell then patronizes John. "You can write an article for us," Snell says.

After John walks away, Snell's assistant says of John, "An intense young man." Snell, though, is more categorical. "More than odd, Bob, individual and lonely. A man who thinks for himself." It's a curious statement, for one thing because it equates intellectual independence with isolation. A further oddity is that the statement contains an inherent criticism of Snell himself. There's the implication that if John, who thinks independently, has a view of the crash event that contradicts Snell's, Snell's view represents the opposite attitude: dependence—in this case, on what may very well be worn-out conventionalities. Snell seems to realize that on some deep level, his rejection of the anomalies in the crash is incorrect, that it is bound up with thinking whose benefits are avoidance of marginalization and membership in a club of nonreflective individuals whose only comfort is not the truth but the company of others who believe in a commonly shared lie. It's as though Snell's attitude is formulated not on the basis of what he sees but on what he prefers to conclude from what he sees, all so that he may benefit from the (dubious) benefits of civilization. Snell actually believes in the inverse of the scientific ideal that events dictate what one believes. He makes events conform to his preconceptions. Yet his attitude is no different from that of the townspeople, who prefer to see the aliens as threatening invaders instead of what they are: harmless strangers who have lost their way.

Just before the first scene with the telephone linemen Frank (Joe Sawyer) and George (Russell Johnson), John and Ellen are out in the desert. "It's alive," John says of it. Ellen responds, "And yet it looks so dead out there." John's reply is interesting. "Oh, no, it's alive and waiting for you. Ready to kill you if you go too far. The sun will get you, the cold at night. A thousand ways that the desert can kill." John's statement is significant because of the suggestibility of its language. The life forms in the desert to which he's referring are actually the town's residents, who may seem harmless and passive but who are quite deadly, prepared to murder you if you go too far beyond their way of thinking, perhaps by blasting you with the sun of gunfire, perhaps freezing you out of their society and thrusting you into the darkness of marginalization. They're a group of people who are creative in only one sense: their ability to draw upon multitudinous ways to destroy those whom they characterize as "Others." This metaphoric desert is really the wasteland in which humans devoid of imagination and tolerance have chosen to live. In truth, it's the townspeople who live outside the city of civilization, and John, out there in his literal desert, who lives in the civilized city of compassion and humanism.

When John talks to Frank and George's alien doubles, who have come into town for supplies, and who are standing in the shadowy recesses of a doorway, John asks the aliens what they want. "Give us time," Frank's double says. "Time or terrible things will happen. Things so terrible you have yet to dream of them." This is certainly not the attitude that the aliens exhibited when they first landed. Then, they were reclusive and nonconfrontational. Now, they feel trapped and threatened. Essentially, the aliens' attitude has been polluted by those of the town's residents. As a result, they have begun emulating some of humans' worst qualities: unwarranted fear and hostility. By the time that they threaten John, the aliens have changed from victims to abusers, a fact that tells us how unreasonable situations can spiral out of control.

It Came shows us that the presence of anomalies can bring out the worst in people. Rod Serling highlighted this syndrome in his short story "The Monsters Are Due on Maple Street," in which two malicious aliens reduce a street's residents to chaos just by causing some apparently inexplicable, random events to occur (e.g., a car starting by itself, lights in a house spontaneously turning on). The point in both *It Came* and Serling's story is the same: Americans' grasp on reality is fragile, especially when confronted with things that they do not understand.

In the Manichean desert community of Sand Rock, small-town affability (e.g., Matt's western-oriented "aw shucks" attitude) is a thin mask hiding jingoism and racism. Just as John's perfectly justified view of the aliens is rejected as a whimsy, so, too, is the legitimate right of the aliens to be who and what they are rejected by the majority of the townspeople only because in some ways the aliens are different from them. The arrival of the aliens shatters the flimsy self-assuredness of a community that was supposedly so "sure of itself."

In the film, there is no inquiry into whether the aliens might in some way represent alternate attitudes that could be beneficial to humans. For the town's residents, the aliens (like people with a skin color different than that of the majority) are "Others" that need to be destroyed—hence the formation toward the film's end of a posse, which rides out into the desert, slaughters one of the aliens, and then moves on to toward the spacecraft in a march reminiscent of that of *Bride of Frankenstein*'s crazed villagers storming Henry Frankenstein's laboratory.

It Came also subtly critiques the tendency of traditionalists to resort to traditional attitudes, such as devotion to one's occupation in the midst of a situation in which unusual events are dictating a complete reevaluation of the way that one views not only scientific truth but the nature of reality. Matt repeatedly tells John that Ellen is derelict in her duties to her employer. "Ellen should be teaching," he says at one point. (He later says, "She needs her job.") Perhaps one of the clearest elucidations of the conflict between John and the townspeople's point of view occurs in the scene in which John and

Matt have a discussion out in the desert. Matt says, "This town doesn't understand you poking around out here in the desert, squinting up at the stars. And now you come up with this story [about a spaceship]." John's response evidences a rare quality for him: anger. "This town! The reason I came out here to the desert was to get away from that kind of thinking." The milieu that Matt represents, against which John reacts, is the same one that predominates in the Santa Mira of *Invasion of the Body Snatchers*: the stultifying conformity of a small town, with two notable differences, though. *It Came* not only goes into detail about the effects of prejudice but its central character does not undergo the exaggerated psychological breakdown that *Invasion*'s Miles does. *It Came* highlights a perfectly rational response to bigotry.

The important point that both of these films make is that this prejudice is no longer restricted to small towns, which now stand as microcosmic representations for an entire nation that has become small in its thinking, especially with regard to its ability to respond rationally and sympathetically to anomalous events—in particular, to invasions of its claustrophobic view of reality and the world. Ironically, it's Matt—the organizer of the film's posse, and the driving force behind the murder of one of the aliens—who gives voice to exactly what effect an inquiry into things beyond what is already known has on Americans. "John, you frighten [the townspeople], and what frightens them they're against, one way or another." What Matt doesn't comment on, perhaps because he has not tried to analyze the situation, is why anomalies should be frightening rather than fascinating. The only explanation can be that in some way, anomalies threaten people who are not only insecure but whose senses of adventure and inquiry have been destroyed.

Also cited in the film is the manner in which fear can be used to achieve control. Although the film's posse is led by the town's sheriff, it's still a lawless mob. What we see in the posse's behavior is a chilling reflection of the race relations situation in the United

States in the 1950s, during which demagogic, self-serving politicians used Caucasians' fear of African Americans as a way of controlling both groups. In *It Came*, John represents a predominantly reasoned response to the aliens. Yet the film balances its implied advocacy of John's point of view in its portrayal of Ellen. Initially, Ellen was just as skeptical of John's assertions as the rest of the townspeople. Her swift conversion to his attitude therefore seems highly suspicious. Part of our reluctance to fully credit her change of mind is due to the clichéd way in which her character is realized, which is possibly a result of scriptwriter Harry Essex's inability to effectively create a female character. But beyond this realization, it is also clear that with regard to the truth about the aliens, Ellen has a thinly-veiled reason to believe in them: not just her affection for John but her resentment against her employer. Ellen says that she wants to find "just one little monster to toss into the principal's bedroom." This is a wildly curious statement. It reveals that Ellen harbors a deep-seated hostility to her superior and the staid conventionality of her job: hence her late-night trysts with John. The arrival of the aliens gives Ellen an excuse to appear unconventional and create discord, in which regard she exhibits the type of thinking that characterizes the townspeople, who use the aliens' presence as a way to displace their unlocalized hostility against their small-town lives. Although Ellen wants to appear to be as nonconformist as John, her attitude is little more than a pose that masks her resentment of John's intellectual freedom. Such an explanation would account for the maliciousness of her vicious alien double, the only one of the intergalactic visitors who exhibits homicidal tendencies. Where the other alien doubles are exact duplicates of their human counterparts, Ellen's acts and dresses differently. Standing alone at the top of a ridge, dressed in a black strapless gown, with a long, black scarf playing out behind her, Ellen's double is a duplicitous seductress. Like a mythic (albeit, at this point, mute) siren, she attempts to lure John to his death.

In many ways, the desert is also a character in the film. It is vast, almost completely uninhabited by humans, and has at times an otherworldly ambience. One scene in the film perfectly captures this atmosphere, although the scene is at variance with the rest of the film given its lyricism and the manner in which it brings *It Came*'s action to a halt. While driving, John encounters George and Frank (before they are replaced). Frank is up on a telephone pole, listening to the wires. Like John, who also investigates unusual phenomena, Frank is investigating a mystery—in this case strange noises in telephone transmissions. Also like John, Frank has spent a large amount of time in the desert, and has come to appreciate its beauty and its deadliness.

After Frank lets John listen to strange sounds in the wires, Frank delivers the following speech, which is accompanied by very low but nonetheless audible, eerie music on the soundtrack. This music's use of strings invites comparison with the strings of wires to which John and Frank are listening. Frank says,

> After you've been working out in the desert fifteen years like I have, hear a lot of things, see a lot of things, too: sun in the sky, the heat, all that sand out there with the rivers and lakes that aren't real.

Is Frank suggesting that the desert causes hallucinations? Is the screenwriter implying that John's view of the aliens has been a result of his being isolated in the desert?

As Frank continues, he begins to rhapsodize over the desert. In fact, his speech becomes uncharacteristically poetic. "And sometimes you think the wind gets in the wires and hums and talks just like what we're hearing now." Inadvertently, Frank is describing the true nature of the film's anomalous phenomena. From the townspeople's point of view, the aliens' ship was borne to Earth on an ill wind—and now, the aliens have begun to disrupt, not conventional communication (e.g., the telephone) but the commerce be-

tween people's current, troubled ideas and what they formerly regarded as a stable reality. The aliens have therefore introduced a
low, disturbing hum into the townspeople's lives, which has led to
them coming to believe that what the aliens signify, what they are
saying to them, is that they are not only different, they are a threat.

After Frank and George have climbed back into their truck and
begun driving away, Frank looks up at the sky at the passing telephone poles and the clouds behind them. As the sound of a theremin blends in, Frank becomes deeply thoughtful, and finally looks
straight ahead without speaking. He has approached, but stopped
just short of fully understanding, what he just said. At this point,
Jack Arnold makes an ironic comment on what Frank may be
thinking about: he cuts to a shot of the linemen's truck from the
alien point of view, albeit from behind the truck. It's clear that the
aliens are following Frank and George because they want to make
some use of them.

When John finally confronts one of the aliens, he says, "Let me
see you as you really are," but the alien refuses, telling John, "You
would be horrified at the sight of us." John's statement relates not
just to the aliens' true form but to the townspeople, whose real
selves are revealed via their exposure to the aliens. The alien's
response to John is interesting because it implies that the aliens
know what a typical human reaction to them would be, a fact that
makes us realize that the townspeople have no such appreciation
for the way that the aliens emotionally function. The alien then
says, "On our world it might have been different." When John
wants to know why this should be so, the alien says, "We understand more." The assumption is that with increased intelligence
comes increased tolerance, a notion that is also exemplified in *The
Day the Earth Stood Still* (although just the opposite view is held in
Invaders from Mars and *The War of the Worlds*). The problem is,
this premise is faulty. Studies indicate that there is no less absolu-
tist thinking in test subjects with high intelligence than in those

with median intelligence. This conceit about the superior tolerance of people with great intelligence, which is not uncommon in science fiction, reveals a tendency on the part of some sci-fi authors to overidealize the aliens that they depict.

At the film's end, the aliens depart, but not before one of them makes it plain to John that "it wasn't the right time for us to meet." The alien's meaning is the same as Klaatu's toward the end of *The Day the Earth Stood Still*: humans are not yet advanced enough to be sympathetic to alien attitudes. In *Day*, humans are literally threatened: change your behavior or be destroyed. In *It Came*, the threat is implicit: if humans do not improve their responses to what they do not understand, they will never advance as a species. The film's unanswered question is whether or not the attainment of understanding and compassion is something that most people desire. If not, the final judgment could in its way be much more devastating than global apocalypse: humans' acute awareness of their profound shortcomings.

5

WELCOME TO MY NIGHTMARE: *I MARRIED A MONSTER FROM OUTER SPACE*

Marriage is neither heaven nor hell, it is simply purgatory.
—Abraham Lincoln

I Married a Monster from Outer Space (1958) moves the notion of invasion into the realm of heterosexual relationships. This film about a woman whose husband is abducted by aliens on their wedding night and replaced with an alien look-alike is a powerful critique of American marriage in the 1950s. The film mirrors *Invaders from Mars* and *Invasion of the Body Snatchers* in its dramatization of behavioral dysfunction and gives us a portrait of American social life that is less a distortion born of psychological imbalance than a portrayal resulting from insight into what it meant to be in an intimate relationship in the 1950s. As critic Per Schelde has noted, "[The film's] aliens can be seen as metaphors for the reality of the chasm between men and women in a society where gender differences had been taken to a ridiculous extreme."[1]

The problems in the marriage of Marge (Gloria Talbott) and Bill (Tom Tryon) don't stem from external pressures such as fear of Communist infiltration or uncertainty about the future as a result of atomic weapons' proliferation. Marge and Bill's journey into the unknowns of a relationship in which both members of the marriage are scouting out new emotional and physical territory demonstrates that the anxieties dramatized in the film come from a place far closer than political events. They come from the depths of sexual psychology.

At the film's beginning, Marge is engaged to Bill, who appears to be a quite normal American male—that is, if by normal we mean a man who associates with men who drink too much and spend an inordinate amount of time sitting in a bar complaining about women and how the prospect of having to deal with them is very depressing. The claustrophobia of the bar in which Bill and his friends drink is bleak enough. What makes the bar scenes even more so isn't just the sparseness of these scenes' set design but the way in which the scenes play out. There is virtually no action and very little dialogue, and what there is of the latter is comprised of Bill's friends' complaints about their wives and their girlfriends. These scenes give us the impression that in the 1950s, American men's social lives have shrunk down to getting together with other men more out of habit than pleasure, and that they drink not for fraternal purposes but out of despair and an inability to think of anything else to do. Depressed about their careers and relationships, these men evidence no political or social awareness or curiosity. They're mechanical husbands who can't see how ironic their complaints about their wives are given their own robotic status. If there's any passion in the film's universe, one is at a loss to find it.

From the film's beginning, Marge's attitude toward marriage is compounded of both anticipation and dread. She is apparently in love with her fiancé but at the same time is nervous about what their life together is going to be like. Her dreams about marriage are about to clash with married life's realities. This young woman's only relative is a controlling mother. Marge has female friends, but they're all either married or, in the case of Marge's friend Helen (Jean Carson), manipulating their boyfriends, so they have little time to lend Marge much emotional support. And none of these women seem to be aware of how pathological their relationships are, how (regardless of whether they're single or wedded) they're merely acting out marriage fantasies that seem to be based not on day-to-day reality but on notions of what a conventional marriage is supposed to be. Eventually, Marge comes to believe that her only source of comfort is her godfather, police captain H. B. Collins (John Eldredge), whose most important scene shows us that he has already been replaced by an alien.

I Married's implication that if only Bill and Marge could actually be united as a human couple then true love would flourish seems highly unlikely, especially since the film doesn't provide an ideal human world that functions as an alternative to that of the aliens. It offers only one married couple whose relationship seems emotionally and sexually productive: Caroline (Darlene Fields) and Ted (Chuck Wassil). Yet even their relationship seems tainted. We're told that Caroline was formerly a pitcher who at one time was being considered by the New York Yankees. However, she failed her tryout because her pitching arm was sore—not from too much baseball but from wrestling with Ted in the backseat of his convertible. When Ted says, "I could never get the top down," it seems that he's referring less to his car's retractable roof than to part of Caroline's clothing. Perhaps this sexual remark is meant to seem amusing, but its effect is no different in kind from the type of leering sexual innuendos voiced by the lounge lizard at Grady's bar. It's almost as though the unpleasant aspects of Marge and Bill's relationship has infected the entire film's sensibility. If we take *I Married* as a commentary on 1950s heterosexual relationships, such corruption would have to be viewed as endemic to the culture as a whole. Based on what we see in the film, as soon as one is married, true interest in one's partner and any hint of passion disappear. In the film's universe, as long as sex was a distant prospect, it seemed exciting and alluring. But as soon as a marriage is consummated, sex ceases to be an elusive, forbidden act and becomes part of a series of dull behaviors in which any possibility of passion or romance is destroyed by married life's routine obligations such as work, fiscal responsibilities, and house chores.

It's difficult not to sympathize with Marge. Far more than any of the film's other characters, she feels trapped in her life and has no refuge to turn to. Her notions of an ideal marriage are shattered on her wedding night. What follows is a waking nightmare characterized by emotional isolation and lack of sexual satisfaction. Worse yet, she has no one in whom to confide her marriage's details, either because everyone else is too indifferent or self-centered to care or because (as in Marge's letter to her mother) the facts about her marriage are too intimate and embarrassing to share.

I Married avoids depicting Marge and Bill's postdinner wedding night interaction other than showing us that Bill is distant when the couple is alone in their room. However, the scene's prominent mirror view of the room's twin beds indicates that the marriage has already become nothing more than a reflection of one: diminished in scale, and implicitly framed by the restrictive social conventions regarding intimacy to which both characters are subject. These conventions are obvious from the nature of Bill and Marge's lives before they're married. Marge and Bill are sexually inexperienced. We know that this is true of Marge from her mother's remark before the wedding ("You're not married yet"), which Marge echoes on her wedding night. "I've never been married before," she tells Bill ("Neither have I," he says). As for Bill, his fixated stare at the teenage couple whom he finds locked in a passionate embrace outside his club signals his fascination with something with which he apparently has no experience: sexual contact (which is suggested when the young woman slaps the boy for trying a sexually aggressive move with one of his hands).

Since Marge's father is not at the marriage ceremony, we can assume that he is probably no longer alive, hence her reliance on her father figure godfather. The film implies that Bill—who towers over Marge and, at various times, frightens her with his strength—has assumed the role of the dominant male in her life, upon whom she depends. Of equal significance is the fact that she's about to become financially dependent upon Bill. There's no indication in the film that Marge is employed. Indeed, this seems to be true for all of the film's women with the exception of Francine (Valerie Allen), a patron of Grady's bar whose source of income is prostitution. In the film's nightmarish universe, a woman can only be financially independent by prostituting herself, either by becoming a wife or a whore. Francine represents what Marge feels that she has become: someone who has traded sex for money. In Marge's case, the currency that she takes in trade for sex (since the alien Bill is only interested in using her for reproduction) is the marriage itself, which in a cruel irony has turned out to be not only loveless but childless. More pointedly, Marge has prostituted herself not just to her husband but to a misconception that marriage would somehow be a deliverance from what she regards as the oppressiveness of being single, a situation that, as Helen points out, relegates a woman to a life of tedium and work.

In her book *The Hite Report*, Shere Hite remarks on this element of some marriages. "The most obvious form of economic intimidation occurs when a woman is totally dependent on the man with whom she has sex for food and shelter, and has no economic alternatives such as being able to get a job herself if she wants."[2] This is what Hite refers to as "traditionally defined" marriage, precisely the kind that *I Married* depicts. Hite goes on to say, "Some of the women in this study also mentioned the connection between sex and economics in their lives in answer to [the question] *'Do you feel that having sex is in any way political?'*"[3] One study participant noted, "I see a lot of marriages held together not with a genuine desire to share a life, but with a need to keep things financially secure."[4]

There is no reason why Marge could not get a job. Nor is there any reason why she could not just leave the marriage, knowing as she does quite early in the film that the "person" to whom she is married not only isn't Bill, he's not even human. Despite these facts, Marge remains in the relationship. Granted, she refuses to have sex with "Bill" any longer, going so far as to spurn his embrace, even the touch of his hand, and, when they're home, denying him her company. Yet when "Bill," Marge, and three other couples go to the beach one afternoon, Marge sits next to "Bill" as though everything is normal. Apparently, Marge has decided to assert her resistance in private but keep up the pretense of a normal marriage while in public, a decision that not only reveals her conventionality but that also is somewhat at odds with her insistence at home that "Bill" drop the mask of pretense regarding what he really is.

When Marge first realizes that the man with whom she has been living is an alien replacement (after covertly following "Bill" to his spaceship), she runs away from the alien ship. After being deluged with images of aliens (much as David was in *Invaders from Mars*), she faints. When she awakes, she's lying in the street across from Grady's bar. Marge runs toward the bar, dressed only in her negligee. Once inside, she is greeted by what must seem to her a perverted mirror image of her family. Instead of her godfather there is a drunken bartender; instead of her husband, a sexually aggressive man who tries to get her drunk and seduce her. Marge finds a double of herself (as well as her supposedly good friends) in the bar: Francine. This woman's come-on line ("Honey, do you happen to have the time?") is a clear invitation to rent her for a few minutes. The fact that Francine plies her trade in a bar that is located next door to a store whose sign says "Church Supplies" is another of the film's exaggerated polarities. The degraded impulses that are satisfied in the bar (the desire for drunkenness and sex) are opposed to the higher values of the church, which presumably supplies an alternative to sensualism. Yet the film makes it clear that there's no redemption to be found in religion: the church supplies store is always closed.

I Married takes place in a world that wildly fluctuates between overidealization and intense condemnation. Consider the rapid way in which Marge relegates Bill to damnation just because he's late for the wedding ceremony. In fact, for all of her fantasies, Marge also feels some reluctance to marry. Before the wedding ceremony, Marge's mother enters the waiting room humming the wedding march. Marge tells her to stop singing "that dirge." The comment indicates both Marge's unreasonable anger at Bill for being just a bit late for the ceremony as well as her fear that marriage represents some sort of death—in this case, the death of her idea of herself as a virginal innocent. The view of marriage as deadly isn't restricted to Marge or the central male characters. In a scene that takes place at a nightclub, we see "Bill" and his alien friends sitting disconsolately at a table. Two women at the bar keep glancing over at them. "Those guys aren't even giving us a hard look," one of the women says, to which her friend replies, "Maybe they're married or something." One reading of this statement would be that marriage mandates fidelity, but that's not what's being referred to in these women's comments. To them, marriage signals a general lack of interest in sex, even an interest that takes the form of an inquisitive glance. The women are also correct in another respect: these men are "something"—in this case, things that have taken the shape of humans.

It would be incorrect to refer to these women as prostitutes. They're not dressed as provocatively as Francine is, nor does it seem likely that they'd take money in exchange for sex. Nevertheless, these women and Francine seem to make themselves available to any male in the immediate vicinity. If we condemn them, we also have to condemn the behavior of the film's supposedly "good" women. How devoted to Bill can Marge be if she so rapidly changes her behavior from displeasure to passion as soon as Bill arrives for the wedding ceremony? As for Helen, right after she catches Marge's bridal bouquet, she gives her boyfriend Sam (Alan Dexter) a triumphant look that seems to say, "You're next," a look to which Sam responds with a dour expression. Later in the film, after the alien Sam has proposed to Helen (a fact that suggests that the real Sam would never have done so), she tells Marge that had Sam not proposed she would have had to get a job. "I'd just about given up hope," Helen says. "I was reading books about Florence Nightingale, Joan of Arc, Madame du Barry—you know, career women. But now I've been saved." When Marge asks, "When are you getting married?" Helen replies, "Before Sam has a chance to change his mind." Helen then playfully pats Sam on the head, after which Sam looks up at her with a look of nauseated resignation. For Helen, marriage is a trap into which one has to lure a man.

If you consider all these aspects, as well as the story of Marge's marriage disappointments, the prostitute in Grady's bar, the lounge lizard who later stalks Marge, and the pronounced degree of isolation that many of the film's characters experience, what we have is a film whose cynical view of relationships results in an extremely negative picture of middle-class life in 1950s America. The film shows us a society in which suburban life has the same kind of suffocating sameness that we've seen in *Invasion of the Body Snatchers*, in which despair over one's life, one's amours, and one's job drives people to distraction. *I Married* tells us that outside of marriage there is only forbidden sex, prostitutes, and leering criminals who prey on vulnerable women, while inside marriage there is a lack of satisfaction and a powerful sense of hopelessness. But then, it's likely that the film's view of marriage accurately reflects general trends about marriage that were current in 1950s America. As Per Schelde notes,

> In the 50s, men and women were perceived to be natural oppo-
> sites and forced to act—by social stereotyping—as if they did
> not belong to the same species. Men were tough, unemotional,

logical, world oriented. Women were their opposites: soft, emotional, intuitive, home oriented. [5]

The reciprocal psychological development between "Bill" and Marge is fascinating. As "Bill" develops feelings, Marge withdraws. Marge writes to her mother that "Bill isn't the same man I fell in love with. He's almost a stranger." This assertion is echoed when she later tells "Bill" (who, unbeknownst to her at this point, is an alien) that he's like his "twin brother from some other place." Later, when "Bill" starts to have genuine feelings for Marge, she is in the last stages of completely withdrawing from him. As "Bill" says, "In the past few weeks you've changed, gone away." "Bill" has gained the same kind of emotional insight that Marge has, but it does him no good. Although the surrogate Bill is now becoming the type of man with whom Marge fell in love, he still repels her because he's not Bill but a substitute.

The stark polarities in the film suggest that there are elements of paranoia in it. Author John Farrell has stated that

> according to Freud, paranoia occurs when an adult regresses to an early stage of psychosexual development in which he has not yet distinguished the products of his own thinking from external reality. [6]

In Richard Hofstadter's application of the concept, "[The] enemy seems to be on many counts a projection of the self: both the ideal and the unacceptable aspects of the self are attributed to him." [7] If we apply these observations to the film, both Bill and Marge seem to evidence a paranoid point of view. The human and duplicate Bill view Marge as someone constitutionally alien to them, and perhaps even feel threatened by her sexuality and emotional directness. As for Marge, the good qualities that she wants in a man—forthrightness, empathy, passion, and love—are what she thought she saw in Bill. When he disappoints her, quite likely because he is inexperienced and she scares him, she projects onto him her own anxieties and all the negative qualities that she detests: lack of emotion, sexual indifference, an aversion to children and children surrogates (e.g., pets).

It's possible to read the film as Marge's extended paranoid fantasy. Consider the scenario: a young, chaste couple marries. The man works in a high-pressure job: selling insurance. The woman defines her self-worth in terms of being married. On the day of their wedding, a breach of trust occurs: the groom barely makes it to the ceremony, a situation that compels the bride-to-be to regard his lateness with annoyance. The (unseen) wedding ceremony is followed by a short road trip during which the couple is nearly killed due to the groom's ineptitude when driving. At their hotel, the groom is unemotional and distracted. Immediately following the scene in which the marriage is (presumably) consummated, the bride writes to her mother, confessing her disappointment in her husband's lack of attentiveness.

We could regard Bill's lateness to the wedding ceremony as a sign of reluctance to marry, his poor driving as an attempt to sabotage the trip so that he will not have to be alone with his new bride, with whom he probably felt safe when they were only dating but toward whom he now feels a troubling responsibility. The wife is sexually and emotionally vulnerable. She wishes to submit to her husband but instead finds that he does not treat her with kindness and compassion. Hurt and feeling alone, determined not to return to her mother, ashamed when she considers divorce as her only option for escape from the relationship, she feels trapped. The stress that each of them is under causes the man to emotionally freeze, and the woman to become delusional. She begins to believe that her husband's friends are becoming the same kind of creature that he has turned out to be, as though his condition were capable of spreading (precisely the situation that we find in *Invaders from Mars* and *Invasion of the Body Snatchers*).

Freud says that "the uncanny is that class of the frightening which leads back to what is known of old and long familiar."[8] What frightens Marge is not what she has discovered about Bill (that he is really an alien) but rather that what she recognizes in his present incarnation are those qualities that she had dreaded would surface soon after she and Bill were married: his taking her for granted, his lack of passion. In his essay, Freud tries to delineate precisely how that which was formerly familiar becomes frightening. Along with Schelling, he comes to the conclusion that "everything is *unheimlich* [uncanny] that ought to have remained secret and hidden but has come to light."[9] In *I Married*, what comes to light is not only Bill's true nature but the potential hazards of marriage itself.

There's a strong affinity between the three stages of paranoia and the three stages of *I Married*'s story. All these stages can be related to Marge's emotional reactions.

The first stage is what Freud refers to as "*fixation*," which is the necessary precondition of every repression:

> One instinct or instinctual component fails to accompany the rest along the anticipated normal path of development, and, in consequence . . . it is left behind at a more infantile stage.[10]

This stage corresponds to the part of the film during which Marge's buildup of anticipations regarding her marriage fail to find the outlet that she is anticipating: a physically and emotionally satisfying wedding night.

The second phase, which Freud refers to as "that of repression proper,"[11] involves a sublimation of desires for the sake of some kind of mental stability, a reaction that corresponds to Marge's attempt to somehow deal with the disappointments of her marriage by resigning herself to them. The most telling example of this type of behavior is her attempt to find a "child"—in this case, the puppy that she brings home, which she refers to as "Junior."

The final stage of repression involves what Freud calls the "fail-ure of repression, of *irruption*, of *return of the repressed*."[12] In the film, this phase can be seen in the full-blown return of Marge's worst fears about Bill, which she experiences when she learns what appears to be the real reason for his strange behavior: that he is not Bill but an alien inside of a shell that looks like Bill.

It's tempting to read *I Married* in this manner, but I think that it would be wrong to do so. Arguing against this reading are objec-tively rendered scenes in the film (e.g., the shooting of the lounge lizard by two alien policemen in human form) that attest to the aliens' reality. More importantly, in contrast to *Invasion of the Body Snatchers* (in which, as the film progresses, fewer and fewer individuals believe in Miles's story), in *I Married*, a group of men who have not been replaced by aliens band together to rid the town of the invaders. In other words, with regard to the "reality" of their respective invasions, *Invasion of the Body Snatchers* tracks the diminution of confirmatory evidence whereas *I Married a Monster from Outer Space* shows us an increase in it. Although in many respects *I Married* adheres to basic aspects of the paranoid scenar-io, its nightmare-like qualities seem less projections of unstable thoughts in Marge's mind than representations of things in the real world that are nightmarish. Marge is not paranoiac—although American culture, in particular its views of social relationships, certainly seems to be.

Although Marge may be a reliable witness when relating the events in her marriage and town, the film is not. Despite its social critique of American marriages, *I Married* undermines the credibil-ity of its central protagonist, not because it consciously wishes to do so, but because scriptwriter Louis Vittes apparently can't jetti-son his suspicion that women in 1950s America are not to be trusted, that they are prone to panic and delusions. Although the story that the film tells isn't about imbalance, the film itself un-doubtedly lacks perspective. It would seem most wise to view *I*

Married as an inadvertent dramatization of its own psychotic, unresolved, conflicted attitude toward women, whom it portrays in a Manichean fashion as either virgins or whores. If there's any truly maladjusted "character" in *I Married*, it's the film itself.

Toward the film's end, Marge manages to convince her physician, Dr. Wayne (Ken Lynch), that her suspicions about an alien invasion are true. Wayne and a group of men from town go to the alien ship, find the human counterparts attached to an electric device that supplies imaging signals to the alien doubles, and unplug them, at which point the alien replacements begin to die. The alien Bill says to Marge, "Your people have won." One might have hoped for a traditional resolution at this point, with Bill once more a human and Marge once again happy, but no such unequivocal ending occurs. In keeping with *I Married*'s alternations between the nightmare and real worlds (a quality that the film shares with *Invaders from Mars* and Don Siegel's version of *Invasion*), we are left with irresolution. Possibly as a result of some problem during filming, when the human Bill reappears, the first two shots that we see of him are grainy and step printed. These qualities, combined with the strangely hollow sound of Bill's voice when he says "Marge," create such an unsettling effect that despite the other normal shots of Bill at the film's end, we are plunged back into the same kind of irresolution that characterizes a large part of this extraordinary film's universe.

6

TWO ALIENS FROM INNER SPACE: *KRONOS* AND *THE THING FROM ANOTHER WORLD*

Men, though they know full well how much women are worth and how great the benefits we bring them, nonetheless seek to destroy us out of envy for our merits.—Moderata Fonte, *On the Merit of Women*

Kronos (1957) and *The Thing from Another World* (1951) are so complementary in theme and structure, it's almost as though they were simultaneously conceived. In each film, the backstory is the most significant element. Like *I Married a Monster from Outer Space*, these films speak to inner fears. The theme in *Kronos* and *The Thing*[1] is that men view women as alien "Others" who threaten their integrity.

The female leads in these films are much more insightful and focused than their male counterparts. These women know what they want. In this respect, they are like their metaphoric counterparts: each film's alien. In both films, the central love relationship is resolved only after the aliens are defeated. It's implied that for the men, such a defeat signals their inevitable capitulation to women's desires, which they regard as a superior force that has conquered them.

Even though *Kronos*'s story takes its characters from the United States to Mexico, and the film contains a few shots near the sea, its action is extremely limited, a characteristic that the film shares with *The Thing*, where most of the action takes place within the confines of an Arctic outpost. This sense of narrowness encourages us to focus on other aspects, prominent among them the nature of heterosexual interaction. Each film investigates men's fear and abhorrence of women, whom they view as enervating outsiders who either want to "civilize" their respective men or distract them from their "true work" in order to be in a relationship with them. Smarter and wilier than their male counterparts, these women try to carry out what they view as their true function: to get married.[2]

Kronos's Dr. Leslie Gaskell (Jeff Morrow) is a scientist who has been tracking the behavior of an asteroid that has started to exhibit anomalous behavior. Eventually, it is discovered that the asteroid is actually an alien spaceship. After crashing into the ocean off the coast of Mexico, the ship eventually transforms itself into a monstrous object that is intent on absorbing all of Earth's power in order to provide energy for the race of aliens that sent it here. The technology behind the film's alien is extraordinarily simple. Instead of having tremendous, arcane powers, Kronos is nothing more than a moving blotter that absorbs energy. However, Kronos needs accomplices, which it finds by controlling humans' minds, presumably via some electromagnetic force wave.

In many respects, *Kronos* anticipates director Brian De Palma's 1976 film *Carrie*, which is superficially about a lonely teenage girl who has telekinetic powers but is really concerned with the power of sex and how this power permeates society. In *Kronos*, power informs virtually all of the film's relationships. Gaskell often exhibits an almost pathological avoidance syndrome in response to the person whom he perceives as his chief antagonist: his girlfriend Vera (Barbara Lawrence). The reason for Gaskell's strange behavior seems obvious: Vera exerts over Gaskell the power of sex, which frightens him. When he feels attracted to Vera, Gaskell becomes not only physically distracted but intellectually weak. For Gaskell, Vera (like Kronos) is an energy vampire. When he's locked in an embrace with her, you can see his focus on research draining away, replaced by an amorousness that he doesn't really enjoy. Vera repeatedly insists that Gaskell needs to relate to her not just as a scientist but as a woman. In response, Gaskell invents excuses to explain why he has to return to his laboratory. His motive is clear: to avoid emotional and sexual entanglement, which he believes that he accomplishes by taking refuge in the impersonality of his work. Like Dr. Carrington (Robert Cornthwaite) in *The Thing*, Gaskell uses science as a bulwark against intimacy.

The same holds true for *Kronos*'s Dr. Eliot (John Emery), who seems to lack feelings. In this regard, Eliot also invites comparison with *The Thing*'s Dr. Carrington. Each man is a perverse exaggeration of the ideal scientist. They're aloof, practiced at being unemotional and objective, and alienatingly smug. Dr. Eliot has a dandyish, pencil-thin mustache and dresses in a style that might be referred to as conservative chic. Carrington dresses in an affected manner and sports a goatee that makes him seem pretentious, a quality that's mirrored in his affected speech. *Kronos*'s Gaskell and *The Thing*'s Captain Pat Hendry (Kenneth Tobey) are more emotional than Eliot and Carrington but they resist this emotionality, trying (as do Eliot and Carrington) to hide behind their roles as professionals. Eliot and Carrington have fled from emotion. Gaskell and Hendry find such an attitude appealing but can't decide whether or not to take refuge in it so they alternate between dispassion and sexual desire.

Mediating between Gaskell's and Hendry's actions are more common characters, in particular *Kronos*'s Dr. Arnold Culver (George O'Hanlon) and *The Thing*'s Corporal Barnes (William Self), men whose professionalism has not compromised their ability to be emotionally accessible and funny. Culver runs a supercomputer, which he talks to, cajoles, caresses, and refers to as Susie. He's sublimated his sexual desire, turning his ideal woman into a dispassionate entity (something of which Gaskell might very well approve). Barnes is Hendry's friend. He teases Hendry, makes fun of his past sexual liaisons, and repeatedly tries to push him into a committed relationship with Margaret Sheridan's Nikki Nicholson, who always bests Hendry when he attempts to seduce her.

Gaskell and Hendry are sexual complements, the former almost pathologically averse to female intimacy, the latter overcompensatory in the way that he's predatory in his amorous advances. There are limits on how these behaviors can be conveyed in a 1950s American film. *Kronos* and *The Thing*'s filmmakers apparently feel that they can't directly tell us that American men are afraid of the sexual power that women can exert over them, so they portray the men's reluctance as something amusing, making Gaskell's squirming when Vera is being assertive and Hendry's sexual and romantic ineptitude a source of humor so as to make their behavior seem insignificant even though it amounts to a serious critique of American men's fear of women. Fortunately, the films' aliens restore the critique to full intensity. The intergalactic visitors metaphorize those qualities in the women characters that Gaskell and Hendry fear.

There's a wonderful complementarity between each film's alien and its central female character. Kronos is a walking energy scavenger and storage battery. Attractive in its steely smoothness, it draws energy from all sources near it. Like Kronos, Vera is attractive. She is smooth in her outward appearance and smooth in the way that she behaves. But for all her attractiveness, to Gaskell, Vera is less a woman than an entity that threatens to drain him of the energy that he'd like to devote to his work.

Vera is similar to Kronos in that she has prominent characteristics. When she and Gaskell are in Mexico tracking Kronos, there's a scene between them on the beach. Although they're carrying on a presumably dispassionate conversation about the still-submerged Kronos, the sublimated power of Vera's sexuality emerges. Vera stealthily (and rather impossibly given the close confines of the vehicle that she's in) slips out of her clothes, revealing a swimming outfit that she has been wearing underneath. She emerges from the jeep like Aphrodite from the ocean and strikes a studied pose: one hip thrust forward, one foot arched. Then, reversing the chronology of the goddess's appearance, Vera runs into the sea and dives under the water's surface. Obviously stimulated by the sight of Vera in a bathing suit, Gaskell joins her. Gaskell peels off his clothes and (after a somewhat awkward pause) plunges into the ocean. Soon afterward, Kronos is thrown into a sympathetic sexual frenzy (which is mirrored in the expressions and EKG activity of the hospitalized Eliot). The probe begins to feverishly bubble under the water's surface. The urge to procreate that Vera seems to represent is mirrored in Kronos's birth-like actions. Soon, the submerged Kronos gives birth to its nascent form. It rises out of the ocean in the shape of a massive sphere that resembles a gigantic egg, a shape that suggests that it is about to hatch, which it eventually does. By the next morning, the Kronos "egg" has produced a monolith that is undeniable in its Otherly presence and force. Kronos then begins to draw power to it, just as Vera seems to do.

For much of the beach scene (as in all the other scenes in which it appears), Kronos is highly visible. By contrast, from Gaskell's point of view, Vera cannot be seen, at least not as a human being. To Gaskell, she's an alien intent on destroying him. If Kronos is an embodiment of negative capability, a black hole for energy, so, too, is Vera. Gaskell regards her as a ravenous beast that plans to engulf him. Like Kronos, she has a physical force that is at once entrancing and alienating: entrancing because she is visually appealing, alienating because of what Gaskell is afraid that she represents. Vera is the incarnation of Gaskell's pathological, fear-driven idea of what women really are: beings intent on subduing men so completely that they will be unable to resist a woman's desire to domesticate them, which is viewed as a form of emasculation.

As we might expect, there are interesting similarities between *The Thing*'s alien and Nikki. In one of the film's key scenes, a group of scientists is gathered around the Thing's severed arm. The men prod it, take its temperature, examine some of its tissue. Their conclusion is that the Thing is a sophisticated organism with the unique ability to regenerate parts of it that have been cut off. The arm has sharp barbs that need to be avoided if one wants to avert damage to oneself. Most astoundingly, the arm's life is independent of the organism of which it was formerly a part.

Now consider Nikki. In his interactions with Nikki, Pat is constantly trying to gauge her emotional "temperature," her attitude toward him, just as the men on the base debate different ideas about the creature's attitude toward them, with the military men assuming that the Thing is an opponent (just as Pat does Nikki) and the scientists (at least at first) showing a cool detachment toward it that invites comparison with Carrington's attitude toward Nikki. Like the creature, Nikki has defensive barbs: the playful wit that she repeatedly uses in her jousts with Pat, who isn't intelligent enough to deal with her on her own terms. She is severed from her relationship with Pat yet exhibits remarkable independence, a quality that both fascinates and frustrates him. In sum, Nikki is a creature who is as alien to Pat as the Thing is alien to all of the base's humans.

Gaskell's and Hendry's anxiety concerning women, as well as their fear of emotional commitment, are more than examples of their view that women are aliens. They're also forms of misogyny. As David D. Gilmore points out in his book *Misogyny: The Male Malady*, "Misogyny is the result not of a single-sided hatred of women or a desire to dominate, but rather of affective ambivalence among men."[3] Gilmore defines "cultural misogyny" as "an affective or psychological phenomenon based on passion, not thought."[4] Textbook misogynists, Gaskell and Hendry are (to use Gilmore's words) "essentialists, positing a stereotypical 'essence' in women, a basic, immutable, and evil nature allowing for no individual variation."[5]

Misogyny is found in virtually every culture. It takes many forms, from outright abuse and disfigurement of women to rituals in which the abhorrence of women is portrayed. In the United States, cultural misogyny has not only been encoded in behavioral marginalizations of women and laws with regard to marriage but also in the country's literature. As critic Leslie Fiedler points out, stories such as Nathaniel Hawthorne's "Young Goodman Brown" and novels such as Melville's *Moby Dick*, Poe's *The Narrative of Arthur Gordon Pym*, and Twain's *Adventures of Huckleberry Finn* make the flight from women and the civilizing that they represent a central component of the action.

Fiedler notes Twain's conflicted attitude toward society. He draws attention to Twain's "ambiguity, [which betrayed] a hostility to bourgeois values that he perhaps still did not fully realize he felt."[6] According to Fiedler, Twain's hostility was born of resentment against "the abandoned world of obligations and restraints."[7] In Huck's view, many of these obligations and restraints emanate from women. "In [the slave] Jim, [though,] Huck finds . . . the pure affection offered by Mary Jane without the threat of marriage,"[8] something that Gaskell and Hendry would appreciate. And like Huck, they seek comfort in the company of men.

Huck's distrust of social conventions twice causes him to "light out for the territory" in order to avoid being "sivilized" by the widow Douglas and his aunt Polly.[9] The same desire to escape domestication is behind Gaskell's and Hendry's avoidance of women. Each has a girlfriend to whom he is sexually attracted and by whom he is also revulsed. They recoil at the thought that the end point of sexual desire is marriage, which each man views as the death not only of desire but freedom. If they ultimately marry their respective women, they will do so not because they want to so much as because they can't see any way of avoiding it. Unlike Huck, they do what deep down they feel is wrong.

Although Gaskell can't conceive of a way to defeat what Vera represents, he does devise a plan to destroy her robot counterpart, postulating that the only way that Kronos can be destroyed is by reversing its polarity via "a concentrated shower of omega particles." The technique succeeds. The monster essentially eats itself. Given Kronos's metaphoric status, one would expect that after the alien's destruction, what Gaskell regards as Vera's predatory behavior would disappear. In one sense, this is what happens: Gaskell and Vera are to be married. But if we are to judge by some dialogue between the couple toward the film's end, nothing has changed between them. When Vera asks what will happen if another Kronos appears, Gaskell says, "If they do, we'll be ready for them." In other words, if, during the marriage, Gaskell once again starts to feel that Vera is a sexual threat, this time, he will be prepared. He will counter what he regards as her dangerous advances with the strategic tool that worked for him in the past: his ability to be like a cold, unemotional machine, one that drains all the life out of situations. In other words, a Kronos.

Where *Kronos* is a film about a robot that appropriates electricity, *The Thing* is a film about a creature that is destroyed by electricity. Kronos is an unthinking automaton. The Thing acts on impulse rather than thought. The former characteristic is displayed during the interchange between the scientist Dr. Carrington and the Thing toward the film's end. Carrington tries to reason with the creature, complimenting it by saying, "You're wiser than we are." Throughout Carrington's speech, the Thing stares at Carrington uncomprehendingly, occasionally tilting its head to the side as though attempting to determine just what this strange life form is trying to accomplish via its utterances and gestures. Finally tiring of what must seem to him a useless diversion that is distracting him from his human targets, he swings his arm in a devastating arc and tosses Carrington aside.

Like Kronos, the Thing is a unique, perfectly integrated entity that stands in opposition to the humans that it encounters. It has no motives, no malice, merely the will to survive. This instinct of the alien, which is only mildly implied in Nyby's film, is fully realized in director John Carpenter's 1982 remake, in which the creature's extraordinary power and purposefulness contrast with the lifelessness of most of the Arctic outpost members who, with the exception of Kurt Russell's MacReady, seem to be individuals with a very weak sense of self.

The feeling of uncertainty with regard to identity that is created by John W. Campbell in his short story "Who Goes There?" (the basis for both Christian Nyby's and John Carpenter's film adaptations)[10] is one of the tale's strengths, especially in that this quality accentuates the burdens of selfhood that are such a large part of science fiction's concerns. Unfortunately, Nyby's film jettisons this notion (as well as anything other than the mildest implication that, as in Campbell's story, the Thing could take over the Earth),[11] substituting a somewhat different threat: the fear of conformity. Although this fear is common to both the Campbell story and Nyby's film (as well as films such as *Invaders from Mars* and *Invasion of the Body Snatchers*), in the short story, it is more of an implication than anything else. As opposed to the Carpenter version of the story, all of whose characters are men,[12] in the Nyby film, which features both men and women, the realization of this fear is not only a distinct possibility but a reality. The fear is expressed via marriage, which in Nyby's film represents not only the adoption of a socially privileged form of behavior but also its supposed consequences, among which is the death of a man's identity.

Some of the film's romantic interplay may be due to the film's producer, Howard Hawks. Although Nyby is given director credit for the film, Hawksian influences abound: overlapping dialogue, the military aspects of romance, the presence of a strong female lead who dresses in pants and banters with her male counterpart.[13] The action between Pat and Nikki does more than provide comic diversion and romance in what would otherwise be a straightforward story about how a group of people in an Arctic outpost deal with an alien invader. It also serves as the basis for the creature's metaphoric aspect. The Thing is more than the "Other," a figure for sexual desires that are repressed. It's also an exaggerated embodiment of the sexual attitudes that Nikki (and, to some extent, Pat) exhibit. Seen in this way, the alien's remarkable ability to regenerate comes to represent the irrepressibility of the sexual instinct, which bears fruit not only in the form of the seedlings in the base's greenhouse but also in the burgeoning seriousness of Pat and Nikki's relationship. That the seedlings are fed with human blood suggests that they represent human embryos in their sacs, a reading confirmed by one of the scientists, who says that their "breathing" sounds like a baby's cry. The horror and repugnance that Pat feels after he discovers that Carrington has ravaged the base's blood supply to gestate these mini-offspring of the Thing (in which regard Carrington functions as the Thing's midwife) is based not only on the potential for these embryonic forms to become independent threats but also, at least partially, on his aversion to the notion of reproduction. Although (unlike *Kronos*'s Gaskell) Pat is the aggressor in his relationship with a woman, that fact does not make it any less true that he also resists what he believes Nikki represents: the horror of domestication and all that it entails.

The Thing's mindless devotion to continuing its existence, with no consideration for anything that gets in its way, mirrors Dr. Carrington's comparably mindless obsession with continuing his experiments, regardless of the consequences for the rest of the outpost's residents. Each "creature" is only interested in achieving its aims. The alien has no plan other than to stay alive, in which respect it recalls the pod people in *Invasion of the Body Snatchers*.

The alien sensibility of the Thing and the pod people occasions fear, anxiety, and a feeling of intimidation. Yet there is another response to these aliens, one that only *The Thing*'s Dr. Carrington and *Invasion*'s Dr. Danny Kauffman (who at the time is a pod person) exhibit: admiration. Each man respects the invaders' singularity of purpose. What fascinates Pat and Carrington about their respective aliens is that they seem devoted to one idea: existence. In this regard, the Thing and Nikki represent perfection. They are so sure about what they do that they don't need to think about their actions. Carrington's statement that the creature is "far superior, far superior in every way" exemplifies the trope in 1950s American sci-fi films of unconcealed attraction to many aliens' ability to achieve great mental focus, perhaps possible only when emotion is absent. Combined with intelligence (as it is in Nikki), this power can be viewed as a formidable threat.

If the Thing is to survive, it needs to feed on the base's humans, who would then become nothing more than cultivated life forms (in the words of one of the film's characters, "cabbages"). This would indeed be an ironic fate to visit on humans, who feed on animals just as the Thing plans to feed on the humans. Keeping in mind the way that the film implicitly compares the Thing and Nikki, we find it telling us that from the male perspective, women are vampires. Nonetheless, the film's conception of Nikki is conflicted. It portrays her as an independent woman yet compares her to an unthinking life form that is only interested in reproducing. Although *The Thing* ends with marriage in the offing, that's less an indication of Nikki's power than of Pat's capitulation not only to his men's urging him to stop carousing but to the ennui that he's begun to experience after all of his wayward behavior. If at the film's conclusion the alien is reduced to a smoky pile of cinders, Nikki and Pat are reduced to the most staid and conventional of characters, their rough edges about to be smoothed out. Pat is ready to settle down and marry. Nikki is about to give up her job in order to live off Pat's salary—in sum, a resignation to conformity so astounding that it qualifies as a vanquishing that far outstrips any that the Thing might have made happen.

After the Thing has been destroyed, and while the reporter Scott is broadcasting his news story, Pat and Nikki are set off toward the back of the room. The rest of the crew members block them from our view. Has their upcoming marriage marginalized them from the community that has been established in the film? We can't tell, any more than we can know if there will be future invasions from outer space. What is clear, though, is that Scott's cautionary assertion that we should "keep watching the skies" signals tension not only with regard to possible alien invasions but also a recurrence of what *The Thing* represents as the dangerous tendencies of women and obsessed scientists, in response to which the only suggested behavior is neurotic vigilance.

7

INVADING FROM SPACE AND SLOUCHING INTO IT: *WHEN WORLDS COLLIDE, THE WAR OF THE WORLDS,* AND *CONQUEST OF SPACE*

The time will come when not one stone will be left on another; every one of them will be thrown down.—Luke 21:6 (New International Version)

In the other 1950s science fiction films in this book, the invasions represent a threat to the integrity of a nation, a community, or an individual. Although these invasions are portrayed factually, they are best understood suggestively. For example, in *Invasion of the Body Snatchers*, the invaders aren't just replacing humans. They're also substituting a belief system that is at odds with the one held by the film's central characters. This approach to storytelling is also present in the 1952 sci-fi film *Red Planet Mars*, in which the Martians have embraced ideas about communalism. In this film, though, conceptual suggestibility has vanished. The aliens are less otherworldly creatures than embodiments of a certain political attitude—in this case, utopians.

Many of producer George Pal's science fiction films take a similar approach, but they're very interesting given the consistent attitude toward religion that they exhibit. One of Pal's chief concerns in these films is portraying his Catholic faith, which he often expresses through stories about apocalypse. In *When Worlds Collide* (1951) and *The War of the Worlds* (1953), the fate of Earth is at stake. Most of *Conquest of Space*'s (1955) action takes place in a controlled scientific environment, but as we'll see, after the spaceship's crew lands on Mars, multiple cataclysms occur. In all three films, Pal uses apocalyptic Christianity to tell didactic stories.

Facts from Pal's biography help us to see why he developed this orientation. During the 1930s, Pal worked in Germany but left when Hitler was elected chancellor in 1933. Pal moved to Prague, then France, then Holland. After the Nazi invasion of Poland in 1939, he immigrated to the United States. The itinerant aspect of his life is echoed in the 1950s science fiction films that he produced, many of which feature displacements of large populations in the face of a cataclysm.

Along with his political experiences, Pal's religion contributed to his Manichean viewpoint, within which the world is divided into two camps: those who are good and those who are evil, those who are redeemed and those who are damned. He's also prone to make films that rework the story of the of biblical war in heaven between God and Lucifer, which in Pal's 1950s science fiction films takes the form of conflicts between godless foreign invaders that are opposed by patriotic, domestic defenders of the faith. These films are often filled with attitudes involving fear of others, apocalyptic thinking, and the belief that the only way in which humans can be reformed is if they are first threatened with complete destruction. Granted, the latter notion is also true of Klaatu's mission in *The Day the Earth Stood Still*. In that film, though, Klaatu's character is well drawn and credible. By contrast, the humans in Pal's films are often little more than stereotypical embodiments of ideas. The fact that Pal insistently links his "good" characters with religion, and places in his films religious doctrines that are conveyed in a heavy-handed fashion, only tends to worsen the situation.

In *When Worlds Collide* and *The War of the Worlds*, respectively, not only are two planets on a collision course or two political points of view but, as in *Conquest of Space*, two philosophies of life: spiritual and material. *When Worlds Collide*'s religious point of view is evident from its opening, which features Bible-style citations about the destruction of Earth; the film's obvious appropriation of the story of Noah; and, at the film's end, a religiously tinged deliverance. Nonetheless, there is a significant problem with the film that is also true of *The War of the Worlds*: Where are the major human infractions that justify the destruction of an entire planet? Granted, it is not unusual for religious texts to use cataclysms as expressions of God's impatience with human shortcomings, but these events are only periodic throughout the Bible. In Pal's work, there is a recurrent focus on Armageddon and God's wrath, along with the strong suggestion that destruction is a foregone conclusion. A comparable anger underlies the story of *The Day the Earth Stood Still*, albeit with an important distinction: Klaatu gives humans the option to reform their behavior. Nonetheless, the implication in Pal's sci-fi films and *Day* is that humans are incapable of redeeming themselves without an otherworldly intervention that threatens them with extinction. In *War* and *Conquest*, such a viewpoint would not be so troubling were it not that Pal's supposedly "good" characters are so unconvincing.

When Worlds Collide was adapted from the novel by Edwin Balmer and Philip Wylie. [1] The novel and film tell a story about two planets heading toward Earth. One of the planets will pass by Earth. The second will collide with it. Both the film and the book mean the destruction of Earth to be regarded as punishment for humans' ethical infractions. Yet as in *The War of the Worlds* and *Conquest of Space*, a divine deliverance also occurs. A passage from the book of Jeremiah exemplifies this idea:

> You show unfailing love to thousands. But you also punish children for the sins of their parents. You are the great and powerful

God who is known as the Lord who rules over all. You plan
great things and you do mighty deeds. You see everything people do. You reward each of them for the way they live and for
the things they do.[2]

In Balmer and Wylie's book, these aspects of God are most
tellingly expressed by Eve Hendron, the daughter of scientist Cole
Hendron.[3] In the impending destruction of Earth, Eve sees a replay-
ing of the section of the book of Daniel in which the rich and self-
indulgent King Belshazzar is humbled:[4]

Belshazzar the king made a great feast to a thousand of his lords,
and drank wine before the thousand.

Belshazzar, whiles he tasted the wine, commanded to bring
the golden and silver vessels which his father Nebuchadnezzar
had taken out of the temple which was in Jerusalem; that the
king, and his princes, his wives, and his concubines, might drink
therein.

Then they brought the golden vessels that were taken out of
the temple of the house of God which was at Jerusalem; and the
king, and his princes, his wives, and his concubines, drank in
them. . . .

In the same hour came forth fingers of a man's hand, and
wrote over against the candlestick upon the plaister of the wall
of the king's palace: and the king saw the part of the hand that
wrote.

Then the king's countenance was changed, and his thoughts
troubled him, so that the joints of his loins were loosed, and his
knees smote one against another.[5]

After being summoned by Belshazzar, Daniel first levies an ac-
cusation against the king that mirrors Pal's attitude toward human
excesses:

And thou . . . O Belshazzar, hast not humbled thine heart. . . .

But hast lifted up thyself against the Lord of heaven; and
they have brought the vessels of his house before thee, and thou,
and thy lords, thy wives, and thy concubines, have drunk wine

in them; and thou hast praised the gods of silver, and gold, of brass, iron, wood, and stone, which see not, nor hear, nor know: and the God in whose hand thy breath is, and whose are all thy ways, hast thou not glorified.[6]

Daniel then offers his interpretation of the writing on the king's wall:

And this is the writing that was written, MENE, MENE, TEK-EL, UPHARSIN.
This is the interpretation of the thing: MENE; God hath numbered thy kingdom, and finished it.
TEKEL; Thou art weighed in the balances, and art found wanting.
PERES; Thy kingdom is divided, and given to the Medes and Persians. . . .
In that night was Belshazzar the king of the Chaldeans slain.[7]

By contrast, both the book and film versions of *When Worlds Collide* hold out salvation for some of Earth's humans (as do the films *The War of the Worlds* and *Conquest of Space*). At one point in the book, Eve asks her friend Tony, "Do you believe in God?" When he answers, "What's that got to do with [the two planets hurtling toward Earth]?" Eve replies,

So much that this has got me thinking about God again, Tony. God—the God of our fathers—the God of the Old Testament, Tony; the God who did things and meant something; the God of wrath and vengeance, but the God who also could be merciful to men. For He's sending two worlds to us, Tony, not one—not just the one that will destroy us. He's sending the world that may save us, too![8]

What Eve means by that last statement is that of the two planets approaching Earth, only one, Bronson Alpha, will collide with Earth. The other planet (Bronson Beta) will pass close enough to Earth so that a rocket containing people, plants, and animals might be able to land on the planet as it passes by.[9] This is exactly what happens in the book and film versions of the story.

Dave Randall (Richard Derr) is a pilot who doesn't care how he makes his money as long as he is paid well. When we meet him at the film's beginning, he is kissing a young woman and piloting his plane at the same time. His insouciant bravado during his conversation with the control tower, combined with the woman's sexual aggressiveness, makes the scriptwriter's intentions plain: we're meant to see Dave as a reckless lothario. Not only that, but he's a liar. Speaking to the scientists for whom he is supposed to transport information about impending planetary collisions, he explains that he was late for their meeting because he had "a friend's aunt for a passenger" and he "had to get the old lady home."

Although Dave never fully appreciates the import of the world's end (because, as Pal has designed the film, Dave doesn't have religion), he comes close to understanding the significance of the impending apocalypse thanks to his falling in love with Joyce Hendron (Barbara Rush), the daughter of Dr. Cole Hendron (Larry Keating), who is heading the project to build a spaceship/ark that will take a select few to a new world. This love becomes so all-encompassing, so pure, that this formerly egocentric playboy is even willing to remain behind on Earth so that the ship won't have to carry too much weight. Pal implies that the higher values that Dave here exhibits only come when one is facing death, a fact that severely compromises these values' significance (much as does the "faith" of someone who, a la Pascal's wager, would believe in God only because the consequences of not doing so are too horrible to consider). Clearly, such a self-serving attitude (exemplified through industrialist Sydney Stanton [John Hoyt], who completes the financing of the rocket because he "doesn't relish the idea of dying") is as objectionable as the materialistic impulses that *When Worlds Collide* means to condemn.

The saving of the rocket's passengers becomes a metaphoric saving of humanity's soul, making possible the promise of a new life on a world unsullied by the greed and abusiveness that, in Pal's view, have caused the destruction of Earth. The film is meant to demonstrate that when human excesses become too egregious, divine justice—swift and merciless—must necessarily follow. While it's true that the film does not state this view (it expresses the doomsday scenario in purely astronomical terms), Pal nonetheless stacks the deck in favor of a fundamentalist reading of the fate that is being visited upon humanity. This aspect is present not only in *When Worlds Collide*'s repeated insistence on secular redemption as a figure for religious redemption but also via its Manichean characterizations, with satanically evil characters such as Stanton opposed to good characters such as Randall, Joyce, a young couple who at one point are threatened with separation, and, most objectionably, a boy who suddenly becomes a member of the departing group and who takes along with him a foundling puppy. If any more maudlin symbols for what is good in people could be found, I can't conceive of them.

Pal doesn't seem to realize that the thinness of these characterizations cheapens the validity of the film's didacticism. Such facile characterization is also present in his films *Destination Moon* (1950) and *Conquest of Space*, in which characters even more incredible appear, especially *Destination*'s Joe Sweeney (Dick Wesson) and *Conquest*'s Jackie Siegle (Phil Foster), two ethnic New Yorkers (the latter obviously Jewish) whose ham-handed behavior is wildly stereotypical.

Moreover, the story of *When Worlds Collide* significantly compromises its plea for ethical behavior. Dr. Hendron includes Randall among those who will go on the voyage (the rest of the passengers have had to take their chances in a lottery for seats on the ship), not because Randall is strategic to the mission but because Randall and Hendron's daughter are in love. "I'll even admit my

motive [to include you on the passenger list] was a selfish one, but
Joyce is pretty important to me," Hendron says. Yet isn't the whole
point of the film's story that in the context of global apocalypse,
such petty concerns are inappropriate, that people are supposed to
rise above them? It is therefore all the more astounding that a
second character in the film also uses subterfuge so that Randall
will be on the flight. Joyce's former boyfriend, Dr. Tony Drake
(Peter Hansen), misrepresents Hendron's medical condition to Randall, telling him that Hendron won't be able to survive the flight,
and that Randall is the only one qualified to take his place as
captain. Eventually, Randall becomes aware of the deception. "You
invented [Hendron's] cardiographs for my benefit," Randall tells
Drake, to which the doctor replies, "Yours and Joyce's." Like Hendron, Drake couches a selfish motivation in altruistic terms, this
despite the film's repeated insistence on religious candor. As a
disgusted Dr. Hendron says to Stanton in response to the industrialist's selfishness, "Men and women have been praying for God's
help and guidance. Not your kind of hypocritical praying but the
kind that comes from deep inside a man." It's unfortunate that the
film doesn't follow its own advice by avoiding a comparable type
of duplicity.

The opening narration of Pal's *The War of the Worlds*[10] reflects
the producer's preference for apocalyptic stories:

> No one would have believed in the middle of the twentieth
> century that human affairs were being watched keenly and
> closely by intelligences greater than man's. Yet across the gulf
> of space, on the planet Mars, intellects vast and cool and unsym-
> pathetic regarded our Earth with envious eyes, slowly and surely
> drawing their plans against us.
>
> Mars is more than 140 million miles from the sun, and for
> centuries has been in the last status of exhaustion. At night,
> temperatures drop far below zero even at its equator. Inhabitants
> of this dying planet looked across space with instruments and

intelligences of which we have scarcely dreamed, searching for another world to which they could migrate. . . .

It did not occur to mankind that a swift fate might be hanging over us or that from the blackness of outer space we were being scrutinized and studied.

This speech, by screenwriter Barré Lyndon,[11] fails to include the more salient details behind the invasion that H. G. Wells provides at the beginning of his novel. I have highlighted the differences between the two versions. The italicized text does not appear in Pal's film.

No one would have believed in the last years of the nineteenth century that this world was being watched keenly and closely by intelligences greater than man's *and yet as mortal as his own*; that as men busied themselves about their various concerns they were scrutinized and studied, *perhaps almost as narrowly as a man with a microscope might scrutinize the transient creatures that swarm and multiply in a drop of water. With infinite complacency men went to and fro over this globe about their little affairs, serene in their assurance of their empire over matter.* . . . Yet across the gulf of space, minds that are to our minds as ours are to those of the beasts that perish, intelligences vast and cool and unsympathetic, regarded this earth with envious eyes, and slowly and surely drew their plans against us. And early in the twentieth century came *the great disillusionment.*[12]

Instead of the Martians' mortality, Lyndon substitutes their being (apparently) invincible so as to heighten the film's tension. Perhaps most striking is Lyndon's not including in the narration (or anywhere else in the film for that matter) the notion of human vanity and the idea that the invasion represents a chastening of human hubris, an example of which is provided by Wells when he discusses the treatment of the Tasmanians:

And before we judge of [the Martians] too harshly we must remember what ruthless and utter destruction our own species has wrought, not only upon animals, such as the vanished bison and dodo, but upon its own inferior races. The Tasmanians, in spite of their human likeness, were entirely swept out of existence in a war of extermination waged by European immigrants, in the space of fifty years. Are we such apostles of mercy as to complain if the Martians warred in the same spirit? [13]

Lyndon also omits the idea that the Martians' indifference to human suffering echoes that of humans toward creatures that they consider lower than them in the chain of being. Wells's book brings these ideas to the forefront. Although it uses the character of the fundamentalist curate for comic relief and as a way of exemplifying an unreasonable and exaggerated response to the Martian invasion, the curate's point of view—that the invasion is a form of divine cataclysm[14]—reflects Wells's attitude toward human follies as well as mirrors that of the book's narrator. [15]

The Martians are colonialists, seizing territory by any means necessary. In *Conquest of Space*, it's proposed that colonization is not just a strategic option but a God-given right and mandate. *War* doesn't condemn this behavior in the Martians. The only reason that it offers for criticizing the Martian invasion is that it is not sanctioned by God. And though Wells's book is as judgmental as Pal's film, Pal is incapable of bringing to his depiction of apocalypse the intelligence and perspective that Wells demonstrates. [16] Wells's novel was composed primarily in response to German remilitarization in the late nineteenth century. Even accepting the premise that Pal and Haskin wanted to draw a parallel between the Martian invasion and fears that America would be conquered by invaders, their film is nonetheless completely blind to the fact that the United States had historically been just as brutal an invader as are *War*'s Martians. And that is the problem with the film: it lacks a contextual perspective. When this deficiency is added to its cartoonish characterizations, *War* ensures that its blatantly obvious intentions won't be taken seriously. [17] That is, except in one sense:

The War of the Worlds' racist attitudes could easily be used as justification for preemptive wars against invaders perceived to be as ruthless as its Martians. The film would then wind up not as a document arguing for peace but a jingoistic work that promotes the precise kind of action that the Martians engage in. Yet the film's major appeal is not to American jingoism but the idea that America is a country of beliefs that are so simple and wonderful (and, as we shall see, also approved by God) that to even consider resisting them would be a sign of unpatriotic, blasphemous rebellion. *The War of the Worlds* unabashedly privileges such down-home values as square dancing, soda sipping, and getting the approval of a young woman's guardian before you take her to a social function (even if it is overflowing with chaperones). The film doesn't chronicle a series of military assaults so much as dramatize a conflict between worldviews. It pits a group of soulless killers against a bunch of good old, God-fearing Americans. Unfortunately, what Pal and director Byron Haskin seem to have overlooked in their enthusiastic rush to make their points is that *War* fails to portray humans in a plausible and attractive manner. As for the film's Martians, their depiction is biased enough to border on racism. Unwittingly, Pal and Haskin reinvoke the same spirit that can be found in biased cartoons such as *You're a Sap, Mister Jap* (1942).

Perhaps the most disturbing aspect of the film is the manner in which it not only takes female submissiveness seriously but actually endorses it. It is highly unlikely that there have been many female costars in the history of cinema who have been as weak and cloyingly devoted as actress Ann Robinson's Sylvia Van Buren. Nor have there been many male leads who have projected the strong, silent type as alienatingly as does Gene Barry in his portrayal of Dr. Clayton Forrester.[18] Astoundingly, there is no indication that Pal and Haskin are in the least ironic in these portrayals. If we can take neither the human characters nor the Martians seriously, what can possibly be left of the film's supposed significance?

The film's Martian invaders are portrayed as brutal. They cause great destruction and lack romantic or compassionate feelings. Anyone conversant with Wells's novel would not be surprised by these characteristics. Wells notes that, in line with the Martians' evolving beyond the body, they reproduce asexually.[19] Apparently, intimacy is foreign to them, as it is to the aliens in *Invaders, Invasion*, and *The Thing*. It's almost as though in a curious kind of development (one that is nevertheless endemic to many works in science fiction), all these aliens have evolved beyond emotion (as though it either stood in the way of their becoming highly intelligent) or, once they became very smart, feelings became vestigial.

One of the most interesting scenes in the film is the one during which Sylvia and Forrester are trapped in a farmhouse that caved in after a Martian spaceship slid into it. Scouting out the environment, a Martian slowly puts his hand on Sylvia's shoulder. The sequence is meant to be frightening, but more notable is the tentative way in which the Martian's hand approaches Sylvia's shoulder and lightly rests upon it. The movement is not only cautious but childlike and gentle, qualities at variance with the ferocity of the Martians' military attacks. This distinction suggests that it is only when they are housed in their seemingly invulnerable flying fortresses that the Martians are ruthless. One is reminded of Plato's story in *The Republic* of the Ring of Gyges, which conferred invisibility. Plato posited that if one were invisible, most people would therefore do whatever they wanted to, secure in the knowledge that they would never be held accountable for their actions.[20] The same principle seems to hold true for the Martians who, the film implies, have no ethics because they consider themselves invulnerable.

As for the film's view of religion, it's conflicted. In one scene, Sylvia's uncle, Pastor Matthew Collins (Lewis Martin), approaches the Martian cylinder, holding aloft his Bible (which has a cross on its cover) as though it were a protective shield. The action is an obvious echo of an earlier scene in which a trio of men from the town approach the cylinder while they wave a white flag and a white handkerchief. Should we thereby conclude that the pastor's brandishing of the Bible and cross is as foolhardy as the actions of the townsmen? Yet at the same time, the film would have us believe that what protects people from the Martians *is* religion. Sylvia's story about being lost and taking shelter in a church until she was found by her protector, Uncle Matthew, begs to be read as a tale about religious deliverance. Via action, this story is "retold" toward the film's end. Sylvia and Forrester have been separated. He finds her in a church that will soon survive a Martian attack. The Martian assaults end, not because of military resistance but because the Martians finally succumb to Earth's microbes, which are described by the film's narrator as some of the "humblest creatures on the planet." In other words, what really saves humans is neither military technology nor ingenuity nor American values and pluck but humility. Given the biological mechanism that defeats the Martians, we have to believe that it was God who brought them low. However, if this idea is to be consistent, we must also conclude that humans (who, we are told, have developed an immunity against these microbes) have also developed an immunity against what these microbes represent: God's will.

War's opening narration makes it clear that the Martians want to find a more suitable habitat in which to live. Instead of negotiating for territory or entering into discussions with another planet's residents concerning a way to peacefully coexist with them, the Martians opt for military conquest via assaults that resemble blitzkriegs. Unconcerned with infrastructure, the Martians destroy everything in their path. Interestingly, although the film's Martians wreak global havoc, virtually all of *War*'s action takes place in California, which seems to suggest that the actual target of the Martian invasion is the American way of life. Early in the film, three men are left behind to keep watch on the first Martian capsule, which they mistakenly believe to be a meteor. Soon after, they decide to approach the capsule after its lid starts to unscrew and a viewing device emerges from it. In what is clearly meant to be viewed as a calculated, unemotional response to a simple attempt at greeting, the Martians destroy the men with a ray blast. Immediately after the blast, Haskin cuts to a square dance in town. The juxtaposition of scenes makes it clear that the Martian ray attacked not only individual humans but also what the three men and the people at the dance stand for: the homey folksiness of American culture, within which even an intelligent nuclear scientist such as Forrester—a man who had been featured on the cover of *Time* magazine and had worked at the Oak Ridge research facility—isn't above putting on jeans, a plaid shirt, and a string tie, and going to a square dance, during which he trades quips with the locals while drinking Coca-Cola through a straw.

Just as curious is the film's conception of the Martians' mental capabilities. Despite the fact that they are described as having "instruments and intelligences of which we have scarcely dreamed," the Martians, with all of their supposedly wondrous technology (which includes devices that can break the atomic bonds of matter), search only within their galaxy for another world to conquer. Apparently, "all the worlds they could see and study" (to quote the film's narrator) are limited to planets within their own solar system.

Despite its advocacy of religion, Pal's *The War of the Worlds* shows us that people turn to it only after all modes of resistance to the Martians have been exhausted. Toward the film's end, churches are the only prominent buildings still standing, virtually all large secular structures having been destroyed. Now, I am not unaware of the fact that many 1950s sci-fi films have a tendency toward exaggerated or oversimplified ideas. In this regard, perhaps some of what occurs in *The War of the Worlds* should be excused. The difficulty in forgiving the film's lapses and excesses is that by promoting a fundamentalist religious position, it invites a fundamentalist critique. And while the film does try to offer an equitable view of the Martians via Forrester's statement that "everything human doesn't have to look like you and me," this attitude disappears once the Martian attacks begin. We are thus left with an apparently insoluble dilemma: *The War of the Worlds* depicts cataclysm on both global and individual levels without establishing a credible connection between the two realms.

Conquest of Space occasionally appears to be critical of fundamentalism, although if we examine the film closely, we see that its religious attitudes are just as exaggerated as those in *The War of the Worlds* and *When Worlds Collide. Conquest of Space*'s central character, General Merritt (Walter Brooke), concludes that the mission to Mars of which he is a part represents a violation of God's plan for the cosmos. Seen early in the film casually reading a Bible, Merritt—perhaps from exhaustion, perhaps from a progressive case of pathological fundamentalism—comes to believe that "the voyage is a cursed abomination." As a result, he attempts to sabotage the mission, and almost succeeds in doing so. At one point, praying over the body of a deceased crewman, Merritt cites part of the thirty-eighth psalm, apparently as justification for his belief that one must suffer because of an infraction (in this case, the supposed audacity of men wanting to go into outer space).[21] The psalm's original version (which Merritt slightly alters)[22] contains the following passage:

> O Lord, rebuke me not in thy wrath: neither chasten me in thy hot displeasure. For thine arrows stick fast in me, and thy hand presseth me sore. There is no soundness in my flesh because of thine anger; neither is there any rest in my bones because of my sin.[23]

For Merritt, humans' audacity is compounded by their use of technology to achieve their ends. A phrase from later in the same psalm provides an accurate description of Merritt's condition: "feeble and sore broken," a description that speaks directly to Merritt's fatigue, for which he is repeatedly seen taking some sort of potion. Like his friend Sergeant Mahoney (Mickey Shaughnessy), Merritt is really too old to have gone on the mission, and is doubtless envious of the youth and vitality of his son Barney (Eric Fleming), whom he has impressed into service on the orbiting space station from which the Mars mission is launched. In this regard, it seems that the problem afflicting Merritt is less physical than psychological, an aspect highlighted in a later part of the thirty-eighth psalm:

> My lovers and my friends stand aloof from my sore; and my kinsmen stand afar off. They also that seek after my life lay snares for me: and they that seek my hurt speak mischievous things, and imagine deceits all the day long.

The paranoid attitude reflected in this portion of the psalm is reflected in Merritt's behavior. It is no coincidence that his suspicion of others on the mission is simultaneous with his belief that the mission is cursed. Is Pal telling us that judgmental fundamentalism is a function of psychological disorder? One could speculate that Pal came to understand the implications of his own fundamentalism and saw that, if misapplied, it could lead to results as disastrous and destructive as the global events that he had depicted in his earlier science fiction films. In this sense, *Conquest of Space* could be seen as Pal's way of atoning for his earlier, inflexible attitudes.

While at first it seems as though Pal intends Merritt's son Barney to act as the film's voice of reason, in reality, Barney merely substitutes his own brand of fundamentalism for his father's. When Merritt states that humans' attempt to conquer the universe is "almost an act of blasphemy," Barney replies, "The universe was put here for men to conquer." He then goes on to say,

> Look, sir, it can't be an accident that at the time when men's resources on Earth are reaching an end, man develops the ability to seek replenishment on other planets. The timing is what fasci-

nates me. To leave his own world . . . it's too perfect to be
accidental.

In other words, conquering space is part of a greater plan that, it
is implied, may be God's. This "argument from design" rests on a
logical fallacy: the ex post facto imposition of the notion of purpose
where one may not exist, and the imposition of human values on a
realm that may very well not contain them. Barney's reasoning is as
ill founded as his father's belief that he is justified in destroying the
ship and its crew. And yet the same type of reasoning that Merritt
and his son evidence is present in *The War of the Worlds*, in which
the Martians' defeat was also meant to be seen as part of God's
intentions.

The justification for this point of view is rather audaciously
linked with the film's politics. The rationale for the mission to
Mars is that there is a politically strategic reason for going there: if
the United States doesn't get to Mars first, the Russians will. Apparently, the political and religious rationales for the mission have
(at least in Pal's mind) become one. In the film's view, the United
States' claiming of Mars is not only part of the divine plan but so,
too, is the validity of American political superiority. And since the
mission to Mars is political, and must, therefore, involve colonization, colonialism also has God's approval. [24]

It's not necessary to comment on the presumptuousness of these
ideas. What is worthy of comment, though, is the degree to which
Pal's religious views have colored his political attitudes, and vice
versa. Such pollution is only exemplified intermittently in *Conquest of Space*, but as we have seen, it is brought to the forefront in
War of the Worlds, in which the Martians' defeat is not only of
strategic political significance but of religious import as well. One
does not have to equate that film's Martians with the Russians to
see how dangerous this type of storytelling really is.

Later in *Conquest*, the "debate" between the general and his son
goes into more detail concerning the relation between notions in-

volving religious intentionalism and design on the one hand and political ambition on the other. Merritt contends that with regard to the mission, "we're committing man's greatest sacrilege. And we can't stop." It's not clear if by the latter phrase he means that technological progress is unstoppable or that by this point in the voyage, the ship's momentum prevents them from turning around, though it's likely that the general equates both concepts. For him, every movement that brings the ship closer to Mars is an affront against some divine plan. Like the filmmakers' view of the denizens of Earth in *When Worlds Collide*, Merritt has concluded that humans are sinful and hell-bent on destruction. For a man whose entire career has been founded on progress allied with technology, this is an astounding reversal of attitude.

After the ship lands on Mars, the general (whose behavior has now become extremely erratic) attempts to sabotage the mission. First, he evacuates most of the ship's water. He then tries to combine hydrazine and nitric acid into an explosive that would destroy the ship. Seeing what his father is doing, Barney tries to stop him. They struggle over a gun, which goes off, killing Merritt. The curse of patricide descends on the crew, which now cannot leave Mars because they've passed their appointed takeoff time and therefore have to remain on the planet for a year, this despite the fact that their supplies (especially their water) are rapidly diminishing. Rationing is imposed.

In a scene that takes place on Christmas Day, we see the crew. They're dirty, unshaven, clearly thirsty. Mahoney sings "God Rest Ye Merry Gentlemen" as he raises a glass of water in a toast. He also shares the last few drops of his water with fellow crew member Imoto (Benson Fong). The scene's intent is plain. The coincidence of the water and Christmas is meant to indicate that the water is sacramental, and that the sharing of the water is a metaphor for communion. Since earlier in the film discussion had taken place about the aridity of the Martian climate, as well as the possibility that nonetheless, the seeds that Imoto had brought from Earth (which he has been saving as though they, too, are a sacrament) might sprout, we're meant to conclude that what we're seeing here is a Christmas Mass. [25]

Despite the time of season, the crew becomes despondent. Angry over their situation, Sergeant Mahoney says, "The general wasn't crazy. He was right. There's a curse on this ship and everybody in it." To balance this view, Pal has crewman Siegle say, "Baloney. You can leave that stuff back on Earth but it don't operate past the thousand-mile limit. Only God can make a tree, OK? Where is it? Where's the trees and the flowers and the grass? Where's the water? Ya hear me? Where's the water?" It's no surprise that Pal doesn't let this despairing pronouncement stand for more than a few moments before it begins to snow. The crew use the snow to replenish their water supply.

Unable to let the Christmas and snow connotations suffice, Pal has Imoto (who is putting together soil and rock samples to bring back to Earth) deliver the following speech:

> I think these soil and mineral samples will prove that life is possible on Mars. It can be done, sir. All the elements are in those sacks. Even air and water and other forms. Until now, this little planet has been alone—friendless, all drawn up into itself. . . . With patience and understanding and hard work, it could be made to blossom.

Pal then has Barney reply, "I wish I had your faith, Imoto."

The film's mood shifts again. An earthquake causes the ship to tilt. Since it needs to be perpendicular for takeoff, the men are once more stranded. However, using the ship's engines to blast holes in the Martian surface, Barney manages to realign the ship. In response to what he obviously sees as a masterly maneuver, Mahoney changes his attitude toward Barney, whom he formerly condemned as a murderer. Now, he lies about the manner in which Merritt died in order both to excuse the son and exalt the father. Mahoney says,

"It's a glorious way the general died, sacrificing his life as he did to bring his ship and his crew safely to a landing on the rocky desert of a new planet. This is the way the history books will tell it, won't they, Captain? Fitting end for a grand soldier . . ."

Following Mahoney's lead, Barney finishes the peroration: ". . . for the man who conquered space." Based on an untruth, these assertions compromise not only the integrity of the general's life but that of the biblical figure whose story it is meant to echo: Jesus. The result is that what the film intends as an homage to the story of the crucifixion and resurrection becomes instead a blasphemy against these events' significance. Pal can't seem to appreciate that Barney and Mahoney's falsification of the facts with regard to Merritt's death calls into question not only the validity of Mahoney's faith in the general but also the notion that it was part of God's plan that men be rescued from being stranded on Mars. But then, such damaging problems are intrinsic to the type of fundamentalism that Pal promotes. [26]

Conquest of Space makes a reductionist mockery of the metaphoric and psychological elements involved with representations of aliens. In other science fiction films from this era, we've seen aliens invade what were considered to be inviolable areas: dreams (in *Invaders from Mars*), marriage (in *I Married*), or one's hometown (in *Invasion of the Body Snatchers*). We've had *The Day the Earth Stood Still*, a cinematic parable about an avatar who warns of global destruction. Other films have focused on shrinking notions of self-worth (as in *The Incredible Shrinking Man*) or agonizing fear of women (in *Kronos* and *The Thing*). In *Conquest of Space*, many of these concerns, and the fears associated with them, have become aspects of a mission into outer space, a presumably pristine region in which these anxieties should have been left far behind. [27] Once there, what emerges as the greatest horror, the greatest danger, is that humans have carried their religious obsessions with them. The interplanetary voyagers in *When Worlds Collide* and *Conquest of*

Space aren't going into space to discover what it contains. They're traveling there to impose their narrow views on it. In these films, there is no hope for a new beginning because the films' reductionist attitudes toward religion have leached out any credible sense of restoration and possibility.

8

SPIRITUAL ENHANCEMENT: *THE INCREDIBLE SHRINKING MAN*

A man wrapped up in himself makes a very small bundle.
—Benjamin Franklin

Richard Matheson adapted his novel *The Shrinking Man*[1] for the 1957 film *The Incredible Shrinking Man*, for which he also wrote the screenplay. The film is a fine commentary not only on the lessening role of men in American marriages but also on American men's shrinking conception of self. Through the story of Scott Carey, who begins to shrink in size, director Jack Arnold shows us that Scott's shrinking is part of a journey that ends in his realization of how he has spiritually grown as a result of his experience. The most poignant film discussed in this book, *The Incredible Shrinking Man* is neither a tract nor a treatise but a well-dramatized, empathetic portrayal of a man's search for himself and his place in the universe that is not only entertaining but profoundly sophisticated with regard to how it uses literal physical diminishment as a way to talk about spiritual significance. As we'll see, the film implicitly cites the work of American Catholic writer Flannery O'Connor, the philosophy of Danish author Søren Kierkegaard, and a very important concept expressed by the French theologian and Jesuit priest Pierre Teilhard de Chardin. These are weighty ideas to build into an example of populist media. That Matheson and Arnold manage to produce a film that has multiple attractions is a testament to their seriousness and skill.

Jack Arnold also helmed *It Came from Outer Space* (1953) and *The Creature from the Black Lagoon* (1954). The former film is covered in chapter 4. The latter film is a somewhat plodding drama about humans' fascination with the sexual power of relatively elemental life forms. No such heavy-handedness can be felt in *The Incredible Shrinking Man*. Aside from a few poorly executed process shots (e.g., when Scott battles a cat and, later, a spider), the film acquits itself marvelously. Not only that, it leaves us with a deep sense of humans' need to acknowledge their spiritual ties to the universe, an achievement which O'Connor, Kierkegaard, and Teilhard would approve of.

Matheson's novel works on many levels. It's not only a terrific read, it has a great deal to say about not only the diminishing role of men in American culture (a concern that's obvious from the book's title) but also anger, sexual and emotional abuse, and how a person might struggle in response to an invasion—not of one's country or town, though, but of one's sense of self. I'd like to focus primarily on the book and film's spiritual aspects: what they are and how they arise out of the story of Scott Carey, whose body and life are invaded by the effects of a radioactive cloud that causes him to diminish in size.

An important sequence in the film occurs before Scott (Grant Williams) begins to shrink. Scott is a small man—not small in the literal sense, but small in the way that he handles his problems. He's more interested in material things than his relationship with his wife Louise (Randy Stuart), whom he treats less as a human being than as a focal point for his frustration. Scott plays a game with her when they are relaxing on a speedboat: he pretends that he's a ship's captain giving orders to a crewman. It's a telling game, since the boat belongs to Scott's brother Charlie (Paul Langton). Far from being the captain of his own fate, Scott is essentially "owned" by his brother, for whom he works and because of whom he probably got his job. At the very beginning of the film, then, there is a concern with the amount of authority and power that Scott has.

Scott's reaction to a strange cloud by which he's finally engulfed is that he begins to shrink in size. But as he physically diminishes, his anxieties about what we might refer to as his metaphoric size begin to increase. The veneer of male dominance in his marriage begins to fade away, with the result that Scott's uncertainty about his identity starts to become more and more visible. Unaccustomed to self-reflection and uneasy about his role in the marriage, Scott becomes angry. He displaces his anger, first onto his wife, then onto his environment. And as his world shrinks in relation to his ability to affect it, Scott's anger grows even greater. Because he is now a very small man, he attracts attention to himself when in public. He's become a physical anomaly, a walking embodiment of alienation. He feels that he's lost control over his life (as if he ever really had it). Scott narrates both the book and film. His narrator's voice is not just that of a man who is reviewing what he has done before but also the voice of someone searching for a way to explain what has happened to him.

Scott's shrinking forces him to accept that what is happening to his body has an effect on how he thinks about himself. And when Scott becomes frustrated about his deteriorating condition, he takes out his anxiety on his wife, who throughout his dilemma has been loving and supportive. But ultimately, what do love and support matter to Scott, for whom his physical condition during the film's first half becomes his primary concern? Scott can't see that his increasing pettiness is the most accurate measure of his true size.

The external world in the film doesn't change, but the way that Scott perceives it does. To Scott, it's not just that he's getting smaller. The world seems to be getting larger at the same time as what he's focused on begins to get figuratively smaller and smaller. He moves from being just big enough to live comfortably among his house's furniture to a dollhouse and finally to a matchbox under the basement water heater.

Although it tells the same story as the film, because Matheson's book doesn't have to worry about its "running time" it devotes a significant amount of space to the psychological effects that Scott's shrinking has on him. Moving back and forth in time, the book makes it clear that the differences in size between Scott and the people and objects around him are not only physical but metaphysical and metaphoric. Matheson accentuates the reciprocity among these realms as Scott experiences an ever-widening distance between his former world and the one into which his shrinking has thrust him. Musing in his house's basement, Scott notes,

> He thought of them up there, the woman and his little girl. His wife and daughter. Were they still that to him? Or had the element of size removed him from their sphere? Could he still be considered a part of their world when he was the size of a bug to them, when even Beth could crush him underfoot and never know it?[2]

Many scenes in the film show Scott agonizing over the disproportion between his ever-smaller stature and the world around him, which often seems intimidating. Yet even when his world shrinks down to accommodate his size, it still provides no security. During the period in which Scott is living in a dollhouse, he is attacked by the family cat. Despite Scott's desire to create an alternative reality, the outside world can't be excluded. Scott recognizes that his dependence on the physical world for security makes him vulnerable to that world's uncertainties.

Scott isn't just physically shrinking. He's also withdrawing into his mind. And because the world becomes increasingly meaningless for him, he becomes alienated from it both physically and psychologically. The film tracks a series of progressive physical diminishments. Scott moves from the expansiveness of the outdoors when he is on the boat to the confines of his house, then to the more restricted area of a doctor's office (within which there are further narrowings that result from his anxiety about what is happening to him), the dollhouse, and then to the basement, in which his life's concerns (food, water, and survival) become basic. Interestingly, by this point, Scott is free of what now he now regards as more petty concerns (e.g., work), which formerly only appeared to be large. He's been given the opportunity to become aware of a much greater concern: his place in the universe, ideas about which he would never have achieved had he not been physically extruded from his former milieu. The reduction of his life to a series of basic acts frees him from agonizing over his psychological deficiencies. His basement existence become a means of deliverance for him. By getting smaller, Scott begins to deal with issues larger than any that he has ever before confronted. Scott's mind, which formerly tortured him with notions of entrapment and helplessness, becomes the vehicle that sets him free. *The Incredible Shrinking Man* tells us that one can achieve wholeness of self via the self, but only by rejecting conventional notions of how that self is defined. In this respect, the book and film are decidedly existential.

The film's first half takes place on the main level of the house, on the street, or in a doctor's office—all aboveground, all in the light. With the exception of the final scene, in which Scott steps outside, the film's latter half takes place in the basement. Scott has wound up in the basement due to a fall (he tripped over one of the basement staircase's top stairs). On a figurative level, his descent into the basement represents a movement into his subconscious, which makes him confront various entities that have symbolic meaning. In each of the basement battles (fighting a spider, scaling a table in order to reach some food), Scott achieves symbolic victories. When the water heater breaks and the basement floods, Scott is washed down toward the basement drain but is saved by hanging on to a pencil, one of which he had used when he was on the house's ground floor to write a diary about his experiences, an activity that at the time he said gave him solace. Now, a pencil keeps him from being drowned, as though what the pencil suggests (redemption through the type of self-consciousness that comes about when writing about one's experiences) has somehow come to fruition. In his battle with the spider, Scott triumphs by killing it with a pin that he pulls out of one of Louise's pincushions. It's as though he's using a symbol of domesticity (which he sorely misses) to protect himself. Scott doesn't recognize the connection between these events and the objects associated with them, though. He's not yet capable of such self-awareness.

Because of then-prevalent standards about what was acceptable in cinema, Matheson leaves out of his screenplay an extraordinary part of his book in which he makes us see how Scott's diminished size has an effect on his idea of himself as a sexual being. Now that he is small, sex is more than just a means of expressing affection or satisfying a physical desire. It becomes Scott's way of assuring himself that he still has significance as a man, someone who can actually have sex with his wife as an adult rather than as the child that he appears to be. Yet his reservations about intimacy remain:

> He closed his eyes with a sigh. Imagination it might be, but that didn't prevent him from feeling like a boy—indecisive, withdrawn, much as though he'd conceived the ridiculous notion that he could somehow arouse the physical desire of this full-grown woman.[3]

With overtones that imply ideas about the size of his genitalia constantly in the background, the book achieves a tone that is far from salacious and more a way of creating sympathy for Scott given the physical condition over which he has no control. Arnold's film does draw on the symbolic significance of the scene between Scott and his wife in which the shrinking Scott's wedding ring slips off his finger,[4] but the film could not include a far more telling episode such as the following one from the book:

> [Louise] turned to face him. He leaned over to kiss her, but he couldn't reach her lips. With an angry, desperate motion he pushed up one knee on the couch and thrust his right hand into the silky tangle of her hair. . . .
> "Oh, *sweetheart*," she said, bending forward. Her warm lips pressed at his. He sat there stiffly. The caress and the tone of voice and the kiss—they were not the passionate caress and tone and kiss of a woman who craved her husband's want. They were the sounds and touches of a woman who felt only loving pity for a poor creature who desired her.[5]

Although Scott and Louise do have sex, Scott's feelings of insufficiency soon return.

In the book, the beneficial effects of Scott's relationship with the midget Clarice seem much more touching than they do in the film. Before he even meets Clarice, Scott says of her carnival trailer,

> He became fully conscious of the steps that led up to the windowed door of the trailer, and convulsively he jumped up on the first one.
> It was just the right height. . . .
> He moved up the last two steps and stood before the door.
> Breath stopped. It was his world, his very own world—chairs and a couch that he could sit on without being engulfed; tables he could stand beside and reach across instead of walk under; lamps he could switch on and off, not stand futilely beneath as if they were trees.[6]

As Scott says to Louise after this scene, "'She [Clarice] has a trailer. . . . It has furniture I can sit on. It's my size. . . . Just to sit on a chair as if I were a man and not . . .' He sighed. 'Just that, Lou. Just *that*.'"[7]

After Scott has sex with Clarice (an act that doesn't take place in the film), the book's Scott comments,

It was true. He was still a man. Living beneath the degrading
weight of his affliction, he had forgotten it. Looking at his marriage and his inadequacy in it, he had forgotten it. The diminishing effect that the size of his body had had on the size of his
thoughts had made him forget it. . . .

And yet it was not so. A man's self-estimation was, in the
end, a matter of relativity.[8]

We're tempted to believe that Scott has come to an important
realization, but his shift in attitude is an illusion. Scott may say that
"here he lay in a bed in which he was full size and there was a
woman held in his arms. It made all the difference. He could see
again,"[9] but in neither the book nor the film does Scott accept his
physical situation so much as find a different world within which
he can live with it. For Scott, Clarice represents an alternate but
normal world, albeit a world that is a bit smaller than the one that
he formerly inhabited. Scott has not changed the way that he thinks.
He has not come to terms with himself.[10] Although Clarice promises a new life, a new relationship, there's no reason to believe that
the problems that Scott had with Louise wouldn't resurface with
Clarice, and in just as large a way. It's sad but true that once Scott
begins to shrink again, he abandons Clarice and immediately returns to his former psychology.

After discovering that his shrinking can't be stopped, Scott's
collapse is devastating. The problem with Scott's reliance on a
scientific approach to his problem is that even if a way could be
found to halt his shrinking and perhaps restore him to normal size,
the psychological aspects and effects on him of his condition would
still be there, just as before. As Carl Jung has observed, "The treatment of neurosis opens up a problem which goes far beyond purely
medical considerations and to which medical knowledge alone cannot do justice."[11]

Scott's condition has compelled him to seek a solution in some
place other than the material world. Theologian Pierre Teilhard de

Chardin talks about "detachment through action."[12] Teilhard goes on to say,

> An honest workman not only surrenders his tranquility and peace once and for all, but must learn to abandon over and over again the form which his labour or art or thought first took, and go in search of new forms.[13]

This is what Scott needs to do: leave the shape of his material life behind. What defines and distinguishes Scott in a spiritual sense is not his size but what he does with his life. Teilhard comments that the honest workman "must transcend himself, tear himself away from himself, leaving behind him his most cherished beginnings."[14] The result of such detachment is that "each reality attained and left behind gives us access to the discovery and pursuit of an ideal of higher spiritual content."[15] Teilhard might be speaking of Scott when he goes on to say that "the loss which afflicts us will oblige us to turn for the satisfaction of our frustrated desires to less material fields, which neither moth nor rust can corrupt."[16]

Scott's condition begins a process that can lead to spiritual awakening. The nature of this process amounts to a dialogue between the conscious and unconscious elements in one's psychology. Jung describes what he calls the "analytical process" as "the dialectical discussion between the conscious mind and the unconscious." He regards this process as a "development or an advance towards some goal or end"[17] and as something that acts independently of one's conscious intentions. "There is in the psyche a process that seeks its own goal independently of external factors."[18] The applicability of these quotes to Scott's situation is clear. Self-reckoning has been thrust upon Scott by a power far greater than any that he has ever before known. The end toward which Scott is being impelled is a reconciliation between how he formerly regarded himself and how he sees himself at the film's conclusion, when he is smaller than he's ever been and when his sense of his connection to the universe is greatest.

When the film's Scott passes through the mesh of the basement screen and into the grass near his house, he enters the spiritual world, within which his newly realized ego is of no consequence. Jung has observed that "religion exceeds all rationalistic systems in that it alone relates to the outer and inner man in equal degree."[19] Within the religious realm, there is no distinction between the inner and outer person. Instead, what's achieved is union between what one thinks and how one perceives the world, something that Scott finally attains at the film's end. By that point, his ego has shrunk to such a small size that he's free to allow the entirety of his existence to enter his awareness. This is not to suggest, as I believe Teilhard does, that there is some divine plan in the imposition of pain and grief. Rather, as Teilhard also points out, there is a psychological mechanism that begins in response to adversity that can move the individual away from self-loathing or despair and toward a more spiritually productive life.

Because Scott narrates the film in the present, we know that he still exists. The narration affirms what Scott says at the film's end: "For God, there is no zero."[20] Yet at the same time, the sense of continuity that the narration creates undercuts the pathos of most of the film, during which Scott feels that he's going to disappear. Nor does it help matters that the basement spider battle seems to move the film more in the direction of a physical adventure rather than a spiritual journey.

Where the book takes time to communicate a sense of the spiritual, the film only brings up this aspect at its end, in what some viewers may feel is an incredible leap into the existential realm. Yet we should be able to see that this shift into philosophy has been prepared for all along. Scott's sense of physical diminishment has always had a spiritual component, even if Scott had mostly been unaware of it. His outward shrinking occurs simultaneously with a new focus on the internal world. He begins to think about the core of his being. When he steps out of the basement, Scott also walks away from confined notions of what it means to be a self. At that point, his inner journey becomes an outer one, away even from notions of self and toward a blending with the entirety of creation. Scott finds his self in the process of losing it. What only seems at the film's end to be an abrupt introduction of metaphysical concerns is actually the natural outcome of notions with which it's been concerned all along.

One way to gain an understanding of what the book and film are about is to consider author Flannery O'Connor's religious beliefs. For virtually all of her adult life, O'Connor suffered from the effects of lupus. She was eventually compelled to use crutches to walk. In the wonderful collection of her letters *The Habit of Being*, O'Connor writes at various points about Teilhard. In one letter, she says, "Père Teilhard talks about 'passive diminishments' in [his book] *The Divine Milieu*. He means those afflictions that you can't get rid of and have to bear."[21] One can see how O'Connor would have found this concept appealing, but the truncated version of Teilhard's notion that she offers us actually misrepresents what Teilhard says, which in a very important sense helps us contextualize *The Incredible Shrinking Man*'s story. Teilhard writes,

> God . . . has already transfigured our sufferings by making them serve our conscious fulfillment. In His hands the forces of diminishment have perceptibly become the instrument that cuts, carves, and polishes within us the stone which is destined to occupy a specific place in the heavenly Jerusalem. . . . The progressive destruction of our egoism by means of the "automatic" broadening of our human perspectives . . . when linked to the gradual spiritualisation of our desires and ambitions under the action of certain setbacks are no doubt very real forms of that ecstasy which is to tear us from ourselves so as to subordinate us to God.[22]

What can this tearing away be but a form of death, in this case, the death of not only one's former associations with other people but one's beliefs about oneself, all in preparation for union with the divine forces in the universe?

> Death . . . is the sum and type of all the forces that diminish us, and against which we must fight without being able to hope for a personal, direct and immediate victory . . . the great victory of the Creator and Redeemer, in the Christian vision, is to have transformed what is in itself a universal power of diminishment and extinction into an essentially life-giving factor. God must, in some way or other, make room for Himself, hollowing us out and emptying us, if He is finally to penetrate into us. And in order to assimilate us in Him, He must break the molecules of our being and re-cast and re-model us. [23]

This is what happens in *The Incredible Shrinking Man*. After raging for the first half of the film against his condition, Scott reaches a point of acceptance at which he allows his self (already under siege for a considerable time) to essentially drift away as though it were something of little consequence in the face of far larger concerns. By so doing, he discovers what many people, secular and religious alike, have discovered, something at the core of writings as varied as the Koran, the Bible, the Upanishads, the Bhagavad Gita, and *The Tibetan Book of the Dead*: the embracing of the death of the self, which makes possible a total realignment and reconfiguring of the way that one sees one's life and how that life is related to everything outside it. When the film's Scott talks about the atoms of his being, about his entire existence moving closer and closer to the universe's building blocks, he echoes not only Teilhard's concept of the effects of diminishment but Kierkegaard's notion that the self must be "grounded transparently in the Power that posited it." [24]

To reach cosmic awareness, Scott must first undergo a spiritual process within which he finds himself poised between two situations that are best viewed existentially: one in which the secure little world that he has built for himself seems to be threatened, and a second in which an acknowledgment of the teleological has yet to occur. Teilhard speaks about this situation:

> *If we are to succeed in submitting ourselves to the will of God, we must first make a very great effort.* God is not to be found indiscriminately in the things that thwart us in life of the trials we have to suffer—but solely *at the point of balance* between our desperate efforts to grow greater and the resistance to our domination that we meet from the outside. [25]

The point of what Teilhard refers to as "equilibrium"[26] is, of course, metaphoric. Yet so is the way in which he characterizes the movement toward spiritual awareness and self-realization. Both concepts are often expressed in terms of size. The sublime irony in Teilhard's work, which is reflected in *Shrinking Man*'s book and film versions, is that the more one is distanced from the world that one has known, the more one gives up raging against "the dying of the light"[27] and the closer one comes to achieving a spiritual sensibility that is intrinsically bound up with a greater involvement not with the physical world but the metaphysical realm. Ironically, this realm is regarded as having greater reality than its physical counterpart because of the power of abstraction This situation is summed up in a quote of Teilhard's:

> The world can attain God, in Jesus Christ, only by a complete reacting in which it must *appear* to be entirely lost, *with nothing* (of the terrestrial order) *that our experience could recognize as compensation.* [28]

Toward the film's end, Scott is clad in a tattered cloth held on by a string. Looking and thinking for all the world like a monk, he says, "I was continuing to shrink, to become . . . what? The infinitesimal?" Scott has begun to accept the prospect of his own death.

What can a spiritual point of view offer in the face of extinction? Teilhard notes,

> When such a death, whether it be slow or rapid, takes place in us, we must open our hearts wide to the hope of union: never, if we so will it, will the animating power of the word have mastered us so fully. [29]

Scott's last statements in the film mirror what Teilhard tells us about diminishment and resignation. At *The Incredible Shrinking Man*'s conclusion, Scott accepts the loss of his self. By doing so, he comes to realize not only who he is but his place in the universe:

> So close, the infinitesimal and the infinite. But suddenly I knew they were the two ends of the same concept. The unbelievably small and the unbelievably vast eventually meet, like the closing of a gigantic circle.
>
> I looked up as though I would grasp the heavens, the universe, worlds beyond number, God's silver tapestry spread across the night. And in that moment, I knew the answer to the riddle of the infinite. I had thought in terms of man's limited dimension. I had presumed upon nature. That existence begins and ends is man's conception, not nature's.
>
> And I felt my body dwindling, melting, becoming nothing. My fears melted away, and in their place came acceptance. All this vast majesty of creation, it had to mean something. And then, I meant something, too. Yes, smaller than the smallest, I meant something, too. To God, there is no zero. I still exist. [30]

It's a beautiful speech. Still, it's not as powerful an expression of Scott's insight as are some lines found toward the end of Matheson's novel, which give us a sense of Scott's new state of mind:

> How beautiful they were; like blue-white diamonds cast across a sky of inky satin. No moonlight illuminated the sky. There was only total darkness, broken by the flaring pin points of the stars.
>
> And the nicest thing about them was that they were still the same. He saw them as any man saw them, and that brought a

deep contentment to him. Small he might be, but the earth itself was small compared to this.

Odd that after all the moments of abject terror he had suffered contemplating the end of his existence, this night—which was the very night it would end—he felt no terror at all. Hours away lay the end of his days. He knew, and still he was glad to be alive.[31]

NOTES

INTRODUCTION

1. The films' titles are *Flying Disc Man from Mars*, *The Day the Earth Stood Still*, *The Thing from Another World*, *Zombies of the Stratosphere*, *Invaders from Mars*, *It Came from Outer Space*, *Robot Monster*, *The War of the Worlds*, *Killers from Space*, *Target Earth*, *This Island Earth*, *Earth vs. the Flying Saucers*, *The Brain from Planet Arous*, *Invasion of the Saucer Men*, *Kronos*, *I Married a Monster from Outer Space*, *The Atomic Submarine*, *Plan 9 from Outer Space*, *Teenagers from Outer Space*, and *The Incredible Shrinking Man* .

2. See for example Cyndy Hendershot, *Paranoia, the Bomb, and 1950s Science Fiction Films* (Bowling Green, Ohio: Bowling Green State University Popular Press, 1999); Vivian Sobchack, *Screening Space: The American Science Fiction Film* (New Brunswick, N.J.: Rutgers University Press, 1987); and M. Keith Booker, *Alternate Americas: Science Fiction Film and American Culture* (Westport, Conn.: Praeger, 2006). In his book *Androids, Humanoids, and Other Science Fiction Monsters* (New York: New York University Press, 1993), Per Schelde attributes to author Ernesto G. Laura the view that *Invasion of the Body Snatchers* is an allegory about Communism (Schelde, *Androids*, p. 100). Schelde goes on to quote from Laura in note 22 without citing Laura's debunking of such a view a sentence later. See Ernesto G. Laura, "Invasion of the Body Snatchers," in *Focus on the Science Fiction Film*, ed. William Johnson (Englewood Cliffs, N.J.: Prentice Hall, 1972), 71–72.

3. Sigmund Freud, "The Uncanny," in *The Standard Edition of the Complete Psychological Works of Sigmund Freud*, ed. and tr. by James Strachey (London: Hogarth, 1955), 17:218–52.

4. Freud, "Uncanny," 241.

1. SLEEPWALKING: *INVADERS FROM MARS*

1. John Tucker Battle, original script for *Invaders from Mars*, revised September 5, 1950. Script available at http://leonscripts.tripod.com/scripts/INVADERSold.htm .

2. By contrast, when David's parents come to the police station to take him away, they are dressed ominously. The darkness of their clothes suggests their emotional coldness.

3. The film's opening narration (which is spoken by actor Arthur Franz) asks, "What sort of life inhabits [the] other planets? . . . Seeking the answer to this timeless question . . . is the preoccupation of scientists everywhere . . . Scientists of all ages."

4. I put quotes around the term "real-life," and later qualify statements about David's waking life, because the film never lets us see what David's waking reality is like.

5. Sigmund Freud, "The Uncanny," in *The Standard Edition of the Complete Psychological Works of Sigmund Freud*, ed. and trans. by James Strachey (London: Hogarth, 1955), 17:241.

6. The demonization of George and Mary in David's dream is quite characteristic of what psychiatrist Stephen A. Zerby refers to as "normative splitting," which is an integral aspect of an unusual psychological condition known as Capgras syndrome. See Stephen A. Zerby, "Using the Science Fiction Film *Invaders from Mars* in a Child Psychiatry Seminar," *Academic Psychiatry* 29, no. 3 (July 2005): 316–21. We don't know if David experiences Capgras in the real world, although it wouldn't be surprising if he did. See this book's chapter on *Invasion of the Body Snatchers* for a full exploration of this syndrome.

7. Among many other films on which Menzies worked as production designer was 1939's *Gone with the Wind*.

8. The film's doublings slow time to a virtual standstill. Notable in this respect are the reprinted shots of soldiers moving equipment and Martians running through underground corridors, not to mention the du-

plications that take place toward the film's end during David's interior-
ized montage of previous events. These repetitions may have been the
result of cost-cutting measures mandated by the film's low budget. It's
doubtful, though, that Menzies was unaware of their symbolic significance.

9. Interesting distinctions and repetitions emerge when considering
the beginning and end of the film. Toward the film's beginning, after
David's alarm clock first wakes his parents, his father goes to see what
his son is doing. When George opens the door to David's room, he
appears as a shadow. George and Mary then put David back to bed.
Standing in the hallway outside David's bedroom, George says to David,
"You go to sleep now." After switching off the light in the boy's room,
George again looks like a shadow. On a second viewing of the film, this
dark aspect links up with the transformed parents' look when, both ominously dressed in black, they come for David at the police station. But
there are more considerations to take into account. After seeing the Martian ship at the film's beginning and end, David says the same thing:
"Gee whiz!" Toward the end of the film's American version, David's
parents tell him that the boy's story about a Martian invasion was a
dream, but David doesn't quite accept what they say. "I guess so," he
replies. He then adds, "But . . . ," thereby reintroducing the notion of
uncertainty that is typical of not only many dreams but of our ability to
tell from both of David's dreams what reality for the boy is like.
The viewer's suspicion that David never wakes up from any of the film's
dreams is reinforced by what George says to David toward the film's
beginning and end. As mentioned, when first saying good night to David,
George says, "You go to sleep now." Toward the film's end, he says to
his son, "Go to sleep now." Though George's being well lit seems to
indicate that this latter scene takes place in the real world, the lighting is
not very bright, suggesting that David, already half-asleep, may be preparing to reenter his cocooned dream.

10. Celia Green, *Lucid Dreams* (London: Hamish Hamilton, 1968),
121. Not surprisingly, one of the objects most strongly associated with a
false awakening (albeit of Type 1) is a clock.

11. Despite the film's hints that dreams are not real (evident also when
Mary MacLean tells her husband that he must have dreamed that the
alarm clock went off at 4:00, although it did), the closed universe of the
film's dream reality makes it clear that what it regards as real *is* dreams,

an attitude that would be not be surprising coming from a production designer such as Menzies, whose central task is to create a plausible sense of the real from the imagined.

12. David is spared this fate. He enters the underground maze of Martian tunnels voluntarily, as do Colonel Fielding and Dr. Kelston. Apparently, David believes that he and these two characters represent forces of the conscious world that are capable of successfully thwarting the Martians' plans.

13. This motif resurfaces in the opening narration in George Pal and Byron Haskin's 1953 film *War of the Worlds.*

14. Although the costumes worn by the actors playing the mutants (with zippers clearly visible on their backs) are risible, they're also just what a dreaming child might imagine: inadvertently buffoonish but terrifying nonetheless. The mutants are like animated dolls or circus clowns, which are frightening figures for many humans.

15. The DVD Savant column on the DVD Talk website claims that there are four versions of the film. I deal with the film's two main versions, but interested readers are referred to DVD Savant's excellent articles on the film, which are available at http://www.dvdtalk.com/dvdsavant/s96InvadersA.html and http://www.dvdtalk.com/dvdsavant/s691mars.html .

16. It's obvious that the new footage shot for the film's British release was filmed years after the film's original shooting was completed. Jimmy Hunt is noticeably taller and more developed than he was when the film was originally produced.

17. To make up for the lost running time, this version of the film includes a newly filmed scene that takes place at the observatory where Kelston works.

18. Blake says at this point that "the little man has had a busy day."

19. Perhaps Hunt's lack of reaction to what he sees is also a joke meant to indicate that cop or not, he's really David MacLean, who recognizes what he's seen before and hence isn't troubled by it. Truth is, though, the allusion is so gratuitous that nobody can say what's really going on here.

20. At the beginning of Hooper's 1986 remake, the main character, a young boy named Jimmy Gardner, is already asleep. Jimmy dreams all of the film's action. When the Martian ship is detonated, Jimmy screams, wakes up, and runs to his parents' bedroom, after which he tells them

about his nightmare. More psychologically blatant than Battle's script and the film made from it, O'Bannon and Jakoby's script has Jimmy's parents explain to their son why he would dream of aliens controlling humans.

JIMMY
(finishing his story)
. . . And then everything blew up.
And then I woke up.

DAD
That's a doozy of a dream, son.

JIMMY
It was so real, Dad.

DAD
It was all made of stuff that's
happened to you in the last few
days. The sand pit in back of
the house, and the meteor shower,
and meeting your teacher and the
colonel at school, and being afraid
of the new kids because you don't
know them . . .

MOM
It's all this moving from place to
place. We're never settled. I'm
having nightmares myself.

JIMMY
What kind, Mom?

MOM
Oh, I can't remember. But people
do have bad dreams when their

routine is disturbed.

Here's how O'Bannon and Jakoby's script ends:

Jimmy closes his eyes, and snuggles down to sleep.
His eyes open one last time, and he looks at the
clock on his bedside table—4:40.

The rain hits the panes of his window outside.
Jimmy looks out the window.

Then he SEES it—a HORRIBLE GLOWING SHAPE coming
down,
through the rain.
The SOUND exactly the same as in the dream.
Coming down behind the hill in back of his house.

MOVE IN ON JIMMY'S FACE, WATCHING

And now he knows exactly what's going to happen. . . .

Dan O'Bannon and Don Jakoby, script for *Invaders from Mars*, second
draft, December 1984, p. 96. Script available at http://leonscripts.tripod.
com/scripts/INVADERSnew.htm .

2. HIS LITTLE TOWN: *INVASION OF THE BODY SNATCHERS*

1. Jack Finney, *Invasion of the Body Snatchers* (New York: Scribner, 1988 [first published in 1954 as *The Body Snatchers*]), 8.

2. Finney, *Invasion*, 49.

3. Finney, *Invasion*, 7.

4. Finney, *Invasion*, 7–8.

5. Sigmund Freud, *Civilization and Its Discontents*, trans. and ed. James Strachey (New York: Norton, 1961), 39.

6. Freud, *Civilization*, 73.

7. Richard Scheib, review of *Invasion of the Body Snatchers* , Moria.co.nz, http://moria.co.nz/sciencefiction/invasion-of-the-body-snatchers-1956.htm . In an interview, Don Siegel made the point that *Invasion* was not meant to function as a metaphor about Communism. "At the outset neither the scriptwriter nor I had that in mind," Siegel said. "I found it much more exciting, instead of seeing the story as a fascist plot, to show how a very ordinary state of mind could start out in a very quiet small town and spread to a whole country" (quoted in Guy Braucourt, "Interview with Don Siegel," in *Focus on the Science Fiction Film*, ed. William Johnson [Englewood Cliffs, N.J.: Prentice Hall, 1972], 75). Siegel never makes explicit what he elsewhere in the same interview refers to as "a general state of mind that is found in everyday life" (p. 75), but I think it is clear that what he means is an attitude that has to do with the way that people adapt to diminished opportunities by narrowing their expectations. Not surprisingly, despite the idealized view of small towns, they are places that encourage and gestate this precise type of despair.

8. Scheib, review of *Invasion of the Body Snatchers*.

9. Finney, *Invasion*, 27.

10. Finney, *Invasion*, 13.

11. Finney, *Invasion*, 22.

12. Scheib, review of *Invasion of the Body Snatchers*.

13. Sinclair Lewis, *Main Street* (1920; repr., New York: New American Library, 1961), 258. Carol's use of the word "alien" links up with the aliens who take over Santa Mira, who represent the same kind of dangerous uniformity of which Lewis writes.

14. Lewis, *Main Street*, 259. The type of curiosity to which Lewis refers is that of the gossip.

15. Lewis, *Main Street*, 257.

16. An entry in *The Science Fiction Film Source Book* about the book and film versions of *Invasion* notes that "small-town conformity is a kind of living death." David Wingrove, ed., *The Science Fiction Film Source Book* (London: Longman, 1985), 125.

17. Lewis, *Main Street*, 257.

18. Lewis, *Main Street*, 267. My emphasis.

19. Finney, *Invasion*, 89. The change in Santa Mira invites comparison with what *It's a Wonderful Life*'s (1946) George Bailey experiences when he sees what his town would have been like had he never been born.

20. Lewis, *Main Street*, 258.

21. Finney, *Invasion*, 78.

22. Finney, *Invasion*, 78.

23. Finney, *Invasion*, 133.

24. Finney, *Invasion*, 132.

25. Finney, *Invasion*, 133.

26. Finney, *Invasion*, 133.

27. Finney, *Invasion*, 133. My emphasis.

28. Finney, *Invasion*, 133.

29. Finney, *Invasion*, 134.

30. Finney, *Invasion*, 134.

31. Finney, *Invasion*, 135. This ugliness is present earlier in the book,: when Miles and Becky discover that the town librarian is actually an alien. Finney, *Invasion*, 129.

32. Finney, *Invasion*, 135.

33. Finney, *Invasion*, 135. Notice the duplication of patronization, which was present in one of Miles's earlier editorial comments.

34. Finney, *Invasion*, 135.

35. Finney, *Invasion*, 135.

36. Finney, *Invasion*, 135. The comment repeats, virtually verbatim, what Miles had said in response to the memory about Billy abruptly coming back to him.

37. Finney, *Invasion*, 135. Billy, too, engaged in bitter parody.

38. Finney, *Invasion*, 134.

39. Finney, *Invasion*, 135.

40. Finney, *Invasion*, 135.

41. Finney, *Invasion*, 134.

42. Finney, *Invasion*, 134.

43. What prompts the intrusion of Becky and Wilma into Miles's life is a change in status: in Becky's case, her divorce; in Wilma's, a psychological problem that I'll soon discuss in detail. But the two situations are not that different. Each involves a disturbance to a status quo upon which the character depends. Becky relied on her marriage, which failed. Wilma relishes her home life, which is upset by her feeling that her uncle is not her uncle. Miles suffers a violent upset that is just as unnerving.

44. See Finney, *Invasion*, 10.

45. Paradoxically, Miles's delusional pod scenario is intended to protect him from emotional involvement. Yet to play his part in this scenario,

he must assume the role of someone who is quite emotional and who resists the emotionless world that the pod people represent.

46. Finney, *Invasion*, 49.

47. Finney, *Invasion*, 96,

48. The book does contain one (elliptically described) consummated sexual liaison between Miles and Becky (Finney, *Invasion*, 96). Siegel apparently decided not to portray this action, a smart move, because if it had been shown it would not have made any sense in the context of the repeated sublimations of desire in the rest of the film.

49. Daniel Mainwaring, *Invasion of the Body Snatchers* screenplay in *Invasion of the Body Snatchers,* ed. Al LaValley (New Brunswick, N.J.: Rutgers University Press, 1989), 82.

50. Mainwaring, *Invasion* screenplay, 87.

51. Mainwaring, *Invasion* screenplay, 88. In an oft-quoted interview, Don Siegel stated that many of the people he knows have the qualities of pods. "The majority of people in the world unfortunately are pods, existing without any intellectual aspirations and incapable of love" (Don Siegel quoted in Braucourt, "Interview with Don Siegel," 75). Note, though, that where Siegel is using the pods as a metaphor for being inhuman., in relating his story, Miles is not being metaphoric. For Miles, the people in Santa Mira are *literally* pods.

52. Mainwaring, *Invasion* screenplay, 89.

53. Mainwaring, *Invasion* screenplay, 88.

54. Mainwaring, *Invasion* screenplay, 88. In *Main Street*, Lewis refers to this kind of untroubled world as "dullness made God." Lewis, *Main Street* .

55. Finney, *Invasion*, 122.

56. Finney, *Invasion*, 122.

57. Finney, *Invasion*, 123. Emphasis in original.

58. Mainwaring, *Invasion* screenplay, 82.

59. Daniel Freeman and Philippa A. Garety, *Paranoia: The Psychology of Persecutory Delusions* (New York: Psychology Press, 2004), 61.

60. Freeman and Garety, *Paranoia*, 62.

61. M. David Enoch and Hadrian N. Ball, eds., *Uncommon Psychiatric Syndromes* (London: Arnold, 2001), 1.

62. Enoch and Ball, *Uncommon*, 1.

63. This point is also made by critic Nancy Steffen-Fluhr in her article "Women and the Inner Game in Don Siegel's *Invasion of the Body*

Snatchers," in Invasion of the Body Snatchers, ed. Al LaValley (New Brunswick, N.J.: Rutgers University Press, 1989), 208. When Miles and Becky confront Danny in Miles's office, Miles protests that he doesn't want to become a pod person because when he wakes up changed, he won't be able to love Becky, which he apparently feels is the defining characteristic of his humanity, this despite the fact that he is clearly in flight from commitment.

64. Enoch and Ball, *Uncommon*, 7–8.

65. Enoch and Ball, *Uncommon*, 13.

66. Enoch and Ball, *Uncommon*, 13.

67. In Finney's book, the pods, realizing how much humans despise them, leave of their own accord. (Finney, *Invasion*, 213), a finale that Don Siegel and Daniel Mainwaring apparently felt was not only implausible but inconsistent with their view of reality so they reworked it for their film. No doubt with the film's grosses in mind, studio Allied Artists told *Invasion*'s producer, Walter Wanger, that they wanted the film to have a more upbeat ending, which Siegel reluctantly shot. Problem solved? Hardly.

Like the one filmed for the British release of *Invaders from Mars*, *Invasion*'s new ending actually reinforces the original cut's meaning. Just because we hear a character state that a truck filled with strange-looking pods has been discovered, there's no reason not to suspect from the film's released version that Miles is not a paranoiac. In fact, it's quite likely that someone with this condition would imagine a scenario in which his or her fears were validated. Rather than neatly tying up the film with an encouraging ending, *Invasion*'s frame encases the story in a flimsy and somewhat implausible container that, like its main character, smacks of delusion.

3. ECCE HUMANITAS: *THE DAY THE EARTH STOOD STILL*

1. M. Keith Booker, *Alternate Americas: Science Fiction Film and American Culture* (Westport, Conn.: Praeger, 2006), 34.

2. Harry Bates, "Farewell to the Master." Bates's story appeared in the October 1940 issue of the magazine *Astounding*. The entire text of the

story is available at http://thenostalgialeague.com/olmag/bates-farewell-to-the-master.html .

3. Edmund H. North, script for *The Day the Earth Stood Still*, revised final draft, February 21, 1951, pp. 23–24. Script available at http://www.scifiscripts.com/scripts/TheDayTheEarthStoodSTill.html . All quotes from the film that are not drawn from the screenplay are from the DVD release.

4. North, *Day* script, 26.

5. North, *Day* script, 26.

6. Konrad Lorenz, *On Aggression*, trans. Marjorie Kerr Wilson (New York: Harcourt, Brace & World, 1966), 236.

7. Lorenz, *On Aggression*, 247.

8. Lorenz, *On Aggression*, 240.

9. Lorenz, *On Aggression*, 241.

10. Lorenz, *On Aggression*, 242.

11. Lorenz, *On Aggression*, 242.

12. The latter is the theme of *The Day the Earth Stood Still*'s new film version.

13. Julian Blaustein, quoted in the TCM website article on *The Day the Earth Stood Still*. Available at http://www.tcm.com/this-month/article/145423|0/The-Day-the-Earth-Stood-Still.html .

14. Early in North's script, Klaatu comments on how the Earth is an "apparently unreasoning world" full of "strange, unreasoning attitudes." North, *Day* script, 18, 23.

15. North, *Day* script, 60.

16. North, *Day* script, 68.

17. Robert Oppenheimer, "Physics in the Contemporary World" (Arthur D. Little Memorial Lecture at M.I.T., November 25, 1947). Found at http://en.wikiquote.org/wiki/Robert_Oppenheimer .

18. Oppenheimer, "Physics."

19. Oppenheimer testifying in his defense during his 1954 security hearings (page 81 of the official transcript) in U.S. Atomic Energy Commission, *In the Matter of J. Robert Oppenheimer: Transcript of Hearings before Personnel Security Board, Washington, D.C., April 12, 1954 through May 6, 1954* (Cambridge: M.I.T. Press, 1954). See also Philip M. Stern and Harold P. Green, *The Oppenheimer Case: Security on Trial* (New York: Harper & Row, 1969). Biographical accounts from Oppenheimer's associates are in Hans A. Bethe, *Three Tributes to J. Robert*

Oppenheimer (Princeton, N.J.: Institute for Advanced Study, 1967), a pamphlet published upon his death; I. I. Rabi, ed., *Oppenheimer* (New York: Scribner, 1969); and John S. Rigden, "J. Robert Oppenheimer: Before the War," *Scientific America* 273, no. 1 (July 1995).

20. This important scene isn't in North's screenplay. It's tempting to conclude that it was suggested by director Robert Wise.

21. Later, when he is talking to Barnhardt, Klaatu says, "I have come to realize since that your mutual fears and suspicions are merely the normal reactions of a primitive society." North, *Day* script, 89.

22. After Klaatu manages to leave Walter Reade Hospital, we see newspaper headlines that read, "'Man from Mars Escapes.'"

23. The rooming house's other tenants seem like a dysfunctional family. Without exception, these people either use power or react to it. Mr. Barley (John Brown) and his wife have managed to develop a marital dynamic in which the woman predominates. At one point during breakfast, she tells her husband to "hurry up and finish [his] breakfast. We have an appointment with the Carsons." The third lodger, Mr. Krull (Olan Soule), is a thin, balding man. He only offers one small opinion, and is clearly Mr. Barley's counterpart: a man who has decided that meekness is the best defense against aggression. The landlady, Mrs. Crockett (Edith Evanson), seems shy and withdrawn. Yet she, too, exhibits aggression, making none-too-subtle statements to Helen about how she is "not courting, you know," thereby drawing attention to her spinster status in a ploy for sympathy and exhibiting passive-aggressive envy because Helen is involved in a romance. Moreover, Mrs. Crockett is not above lying to achieve her ends. When Klaatu shows an interest in obtaining a room, she not only tells him how nice the boardinghouse is but says of Helen's son Bobby that he's "so well behaved, and quiet as a mouse," assertions intended to get a laugh out of an audience that realizes that she's probably misrepresenting things. She takes advantage of Klaatu's ignorance with regard to the house's living conditions just as Bobby takes advantage of Klaatu's ignorance about the value of diamonds.

24. North, *Day* script, 68.

25. Jonathan Edwards, "Sinners in the Hands of an Angry God," July 8, 1741, available at Christian Classics Ethereal Library, http://www.ccel.org/ccel/edwards/sermons.sinners.html .

26. Edwards, "Sinners."

27. North, *Day* script, 110–12.

28. *Wikipedia*, s.v. "Prevenient grace," last modified May 3, 2014, http://en.wikipedia.org/wiki/Prevenient_Grace .

29. Isa. 66:15 (King James Version), quoted in Edwards, "Sinners."

30. In director Scott Derrickson's 2008 remake of Wise's film, Klaatu's people are more altruistic than in the earlier film. The 1951 Klaatu states, "So long as you were limited to fighting among yourselves—with your primitive tanks and planes—we were unconcerned." In the new version of the film, the aliens' concern with harm to other planets has been replaced with an interest in the negative environmental impact that humans are having on planet Earth, even though in both films, a form of preservation is the motivating principle behind Klaatu's visit. Nonetheless, the two films' psychological assumptions are identical. It's clear to Klaatu's people in both films that humans don't have a self-protective impulse powerful enough to prevent them from destroying themselves. Although in each film the view of humans that Klaatu has when he first comes to Earth is changed as a result of exposure to a humanistic woman and her child, the 2008 film alters the child's character, making the reaction to his military father's death one of bitterness and resentment. This difference between these characters may be the result of Derrickson's wanting to have Jaden Smith's Jacob angry during the film's first half so that we can see a development in his character when he comes to realize that Klaatu is well intentioned, not the enemy that he first views him as.

One of the most notable characteristics of Wise's film is its almost complete lack of special effects. With the exception of some optically printed shots (e.g., the spaceship's landing), Wise's *Day* relies on the strength of its actors' performances and the intelligence of its script to make its points. In the film's contemporary version, the performances are relatively flat. Keanu Reeves's Klaatu and Jennifer Connelly's Helen Benson bring an emotional deadness to their roles, quite a contrast to the reserved but obviously emotional attitude of Michael Rennie's Klaatu and the passions displayed by Patricia Neal's Helen. As for the new film's CGI (computer-generated imagery) effects, they draw attention to their artificiality. In one scene in which a sports stadium is disintegrating, part of the stadium doesn't collapse but merely disappears. The result is that not only is all suspension of disbelief destroyed but so, too, is any emotional investment that we might have in the scene.

4. WE DON'T LIKE YOUR KIND HERE: *IT CAME FROM OUTER SPACE*

1. In a statement that virtually duplicates what *Invasion of the Body Snatchers'* Danny says to Miles after Miles contends that he had seen Becky's double in her father's basement ("You saw her all right, in every tiny detail, as vividly as anyone has ever seen anything. But only in your mind."), Snell tells John, "You saw something that looked like a ship. You can't prove it."

5. WELCOME TO MY NIGHTMARE: *I MARRIED A MONSTER FROM OUTER SPACE*

1. Per Schelde, *Androids, Humanoids, and Other Science Fiction Monsters: Science and Soul in Science Fiction Films* (New York: New York University Press, 1993), 103.
2. Shere Hite, *The Hite Report* (New York: Macmillan, 1976), 294.
3. Hite, *Hite Report*, 295. Emphasis in original.
4. Hite, *Hite Report*, 295.
5. Schelde, *Androids*, 103.
6. John Farrell, *Freud's Paranoid Quest* (New York: New York University Press, 1966), 11.
7. Richard Hofstadter, "The Paranoid Style in American Politics," in *The Paranoid Style in American Politics and Other Essays* (New York: Knopf, 1966), 32.
8. Sigmund Freud, "The Uncanny," in *The Standard Edition of the Complete Psychological Works of Sigmund Freud*, trans. and ed. James Strachey (London: Hogarth, 1955), 17:220.
9. Schelling, referred to by Freud in "Uncanny," 225.
10. Sigmund Freud, *The Standard Edition of the Complete Psychological Works of Sigmund Freud*, Volume 12 (London: Hogarth, 1955), 68.
11. Freud, *The Standard Edition of the Complete Psychological Works of Sigmund Freud*, 67.
12. Freud, *The Standard Edition of the Complete Psychological Works of Sigmund Freud*, 68.

6. TWO ALIENS FROM INNER SPACE: *KRONOS* AND *THE THING FROM ANOTHER WORLD*

1. I use the shortened form of the film's title in this chapter but am careful to distinguish the 1951 film from its 1982 remake, whose title is *The Thing*.

2. Even though there were practical reasons for this attitude among women in the 1950s (perhaps chiefly, the lack of well-paying jobs that would have made financial independence for them possible), these films ignore such considerations, focusing instead on their male protagonists' attitudes, ill founded though they may be.

3. David D. Gilmore, *Misogyny: The Male Malady* (Philadelphia: University of Pennsylvania Press, 2001), 9. While misogyny is central to *Kronos* and *The Thing*, it is also present in some of the other films discussed in this book. In *Invaders from Mars*, David has such a pronounced ambivalence toward his mother that in his dream, he bifurcates her into opposites: One, his ideal mother, is a comforting angel in white. His real mother is a demon dressed in black (whose threatening aspect in mirrored in a young girl who burns down her parents' house). *Invasion*'s Miles is simultaneously attracted to Becky and repulsed by her. Like the female love interest in 1953's *It Came from Outer Space*, who is duplicated by the alien invaders, Becky's double is an evil temptress bent on the protagonist's destruction. In *The Day the Earth Stood Still*, the quality in Klaatu that makes him attractive to Helen is that in contrast to her aggressive and manipulative boyfriend, Klaatu seems virtually asexual. As a result, he doesn't seem to be prone to territoriality or controlling behavior. Although threatening with regard to his political attitudes, in personal relationships with people whom he likes he is gentle and compassionate.

4. Gilmore, *Misogyny*, 13.

5. Gilmore, *Misogyny*, 14.

6. Leslie Fiedler, *Love and Death in the American Novel* (New York: Criterion Books, 1960), 556.

7. Fielder, *Love and Death*, 569.

8. Fiedler, *Love and Death*, 584–85.

9. Mark Twain, *Adventures of Huckleberry Finn,* ed. Henry Nash Smith (Boston: Houghton Mifflin, 1958), 3, 245.

10. John W. Campbell Jr., "Who Goes There?" in *Who Goes There? Seven Tales of Science Fiction* (Westport, Conn.: Hyperion, 1976).

Campbell's story originally appeared in *Astounding* magazine in August 1938.

11. As Campbell's character Blair says, the Thing could achieve this end by "becom[ing] the population of the world." Campbell, "Who Goes There?," 33.

12. The only "female" in Carpenter's film is a computer with which the character MacReady plays chess. When the computer wins the game, MacReady calls the computer a "cheating bitch."

Carpenter's film is far more faithful to Campbell's narrative than is Nyby's. Carpenter not only retains the Thing's shape-changing capability but also some of the truly harrowing scenes from the story: the frightening transformation of some of the Arctic outpost's members; the madness that descends upon Blair; the extended testing of crew members' blood to see if they are human or not. Where the Carpenter film falls short is in its stress on its graphic special effects (which are doubtless disturbing and communicate an effective sense of the men's primal fears) at the expense of potential character development. This is not to say that the Campbell story is strong in this regard, either, merely that since there are such potent visuals in the Carpenter film, and such a striking sense of life in the creature (one of Campbell's characters describes the Thing as having "an unearthly, unkillable vitality" [Campbell, "Who Goes There?," 29]), it's unfortunate that the more human elements of the story (which would have provided a fine contrast to the dehumanizing duplication in the story) are not comparably strong. However, it may be that the absence of humanistic touches in the film was intentional, especially in that this quality serves as a predisposition for the outpost's men to become absorbed into an unfeeling entity such as the Thing.

13. Although only Charles Lederer receives on-screen credit for the film's script, Hawks and Ben Hecht also contributed to it.

7. INVADING FROM SPACE AND SLOUCHING INTO IT: *WHEN WORLDS COLLIDE, THE WAR OF THE WORLDS,* AND *CONQUEST OF SPACE*

1. Edwin Balmer and Philip Wylie, *When Worlds Collide* (Philadelphia: Lippincott, 1932).

2. Jer. 32:18–19 (New English Translation).

3. In the film, the character's first name is Joyce.

4. Balmer and Wylie, *When Worlds Collide*, 71–73.

5. Dan. 5:1–6 (King James Version).

6. Dan. 5:22–23 (KJV).

7. Dan. 5:25–28, 30 (KJV).

8. Balmer and Wylie, *When Worlds Collide*, 38.

9. In Pal's film, the planets are called Bellus and Zyra.

10. "The rights [to *War of the Worlds*] were first purchased in 1925 by Paramount director Cecil B. DeMille and then went through a tortured series of abortive productions. That H G Wells [*sic*] had sold the rights in perpetuity to Paramount did not help the situation. In the 1930's [*sic*], even Alfred Hitchcock, (who was unconnected with Paramount) failed to persuade Wells to let him make the film because of this restrictive arrangement." http://www.war-ofthe-worlds.co.uk/filmandtv.htm.

11. A pseudonym for Alfred Edgar.

12. H. G. Wells, *The War of the Worlds* (1898; repr., New York: Oxford University Press, 1995), 7. My emphasis.

13. Wells, *War of the Worlds*, 9.

14. Wells, *The War of the Worlds*, 69–71, 123.

15. Nonetheless, Wells also has the narrator say to the curate, "Be a man! . . . You are scared out of your wits. What good is religion if it collapses under calamity? Think of what earthquakes and floods, wars and volcanoes, have done before to men! Did you think God had exempted Weybridge? He is not an insurance agent" (Wells, *War of the Worlds*, 71). Interestingly, the curate assumes part of the role of the film's Sylvia: not just her religious attitude, but also in the way that he becomes the companion of the story's central figure. In the film, Forrester and Sylvia are in a farmhouse that is partially buried. In the book, the narrator's companion in an identical scene is the curate. Wells, *War of the Worlds*, 122–23.

16. Unfortunately, while the novel's mob panic scene includes (as does the film) a character who is trying to escape with his money, Wells makes this person a Jew. Wells, *The War of the Worlds*, 101.

17. Pal is of the opposite opinion. He feels that the film's screenplay is an example of a fine adaptation. "Whenever a Hollywood producer brings out a new motion picture in which he has tampered with the plot of a well-known novel or play, he's inviting criticism. We took that risk when we made the H. G. Wells classic, 'War of The Worlds,' but inasmuch as

none of us connected with it have been dodging any verbal tomatoes since, I take it that the audiences approve." George Pal comment available at http://www.roger-russell.com/war/war.htm .

18. Not surprisingly, Pal holds just the opposite opinion. "How [Wells] . . . would have taken our addition of a romantic interest I won't hazard a guess. But in the film business you have to be practical. No one is less interested in doing routine boy meets girl stories than I. But a boy-and-girl theme is necessary even in a science-fiction film of the scope of 'War of the Worlds.' Audiences want it. So we introduced a young college scientist played by a talented newcomer named Gene Barry. As his companion we cast Ann Robinson, another bright new talent." Quote available at http://www.roger-russell.com/war/war.htm .

19. Wells, *War of the Worlds*, 129. In this regard, the Martians are like the Thing.

20. Plato, *The Republic of Plato*, trans. Francis MacDonald Cornford (New York: Oxford University Press, 1945), 44–45. The restraining element missing in Plato's invisible man is integrity, which would prevent him from taking advantage of his power. Keeping Plato's notion in mind, we could read the Martians' blood deficiency (anemia) as a figure for their moral deficiency, and their poor eyesight as a metaphor for their ethically compromised way of viewing things.

21. Merritt's citation has nothing to do with the death of the crewman (whose spacesuit was pierced by a meteor fragment) and everything to do with Merritt's solipsistic fundamentalism. Of course, it could be contended that the pain to which Merritt is referring is his agony over the crewman's death. But even were this so, Merritt is still focusing on himself.

22. Merritt does not include the words "in thy wrath" after "rebuke me not," a strange omission considering how fixated he is on divine retribution. He also skips all of the psalm's lines after line 3 except for the psalm's last line, "Make haste to help me, O Lord my salvation."

23. Ps. 38 (KJV). All references to the thirty-eighth psalm are from this version.

24. In *Destination Moon*, the man who conceives the mission to the moon, General Thayer (Tom Powers), is quite like Merritt. Thayer, of whom it is said that he "crusaded [himself] right out of the service and [then] kept on crusading," believes that if the United States doesn't reach the moon before any other country, it will no longer be referred to as the

United States but as "the disunited world." That Thayer is referred to as a "prophet without honor" and an advocate of interplanetary travel in search of "vindication" makes it clear that his character has been cast from virtually the same religious mold as General Merritt. Not surprisingly, at the end of *Destination Moon*, the moon is claimed "in the name of the United States," albeit "for the benefit of all mankind."

25. In another irony that Pal and scriptwriters Philip Yordan, Barré Lyndon, George Worthing Yates, and James O' Hanlon pile on, immediately after Imoto says that if the planet had water, his seeds could grow, the general evacuates most of the ship's water supply.

26. Especially with regard to these three films, it's difficult not to see Pal the filmmaker as a contemporary Daniel, albeit one who perceives signs of God's presence in many intergalactic events, all of them having to do with disaster. Pal is also quite like the Bible-obsessed General Merritt of *Conquest of Space*.

27. Writer William S. Burroughs says in his book *The Job*, "Anyone who prays in space is not there." William S. Burroughs, *The Job—Interviews with William S. Burroughs by Daniel Odier* (New York: Grove, 1974).

8. SPIRITUAL ENHANCEMENT: *THE INCREDIBLE SHRINKING MAN*

1. Richard Matheson, *The Shrinking Man* (New York: Buccaneer Books, 1962).

2. Matheson, *Shrinking Man*, 12. Note how effectively Matheson gives us the impression of Scott's alienation from his family by having Scott first refer to them not as relatives but merely as other people.

3. Matheson, *Shrinking Man*, 36–37.

4. There's a comparable episode in the book during which Scott's wife discovers that he's now wearing his wedding ring on a chain around his neck because the ring is far too big for his finger. Matheson, *Shrinking Man*, 42.

5. Matheson, *Shrinking Man*, 38. Emphasis in original.

6. Matheson, *Shrinking Man*, 137.

7. Matheson, *Shrinking Man*, 145. Emphasis in original.

8. Matheson, *Shrinking Man*, 147.

9. Matheson, *Shrinking Man*, 147.

10. The book emphasizes how torturous ideas and feelings related to sex can be for Scott. It includes a harrowing episode in which a drunken man gives Scott (whose size makes him look like a teenager) a ride in his car. The man tries to seduce Scott (Matheson, *Shrinking Man*, 58–64). Later, a very small Scott experiences wrenching desire for a young woman whom Louise has hired to watch their daughter. In an agonizing linkage, Scott uses a phrase about the babysitter ("age of pristine possibility") that the man who had tried to seduce him had used (Matheson, *Shrinking Man*, 120 and 62). Although he rejects the connection ("Where had he heard that phrase before? He shook it off" [Matheson, *Shrinking Man*, 120]), Scott subconsciously comes to the realization that one of the psychological effects of his diminishment is that he is becoming very similar to this man, especially in the desire for being young again, which for both of them represents a period in which they were not only sexually active but were in a satisfying relationship. When Scott runs away from the man, Matheson writes, "The man turned his heavy head and watched *youth* racing away from him" (Matheson, *Shrinking Man*, 64. My emphasis).

11. Carl Jung, *Basic Writings*, ed. Violet Staub de Laszlo (New York: Modern Library, 1959), 435.

12. Pierre Teilhard de Chardin, *The Divine Milieu: An Essay on the Interior Life* (New York: Harper & Row, 1960), 40.

13. Teilhard de Chardin, *Divine Milieu*, 41.

14. Teilhard de Chardin, *Divine Milieu*, 41.

15. Teilhard de Chardin, *Divine Milieu*, 41.

16. Teilhard de Chardin, *Divine Milieu*, 41.

17. Jung, *Basic Writings*, 434.

18. Jung, *Basic Writings*, 435.

19. Jung, *Basic Writings*, 437.

20. See also Matheson, *Shrinking Man*, 17, 192.

21. Flannery O'Connor, letter to Janet McKane in *The Habit of Being*, ed. Sally Fitzgerald (New York: Farrar, Straus & Giroux, 1979), 509.

22. Teilhard de Chardin, *Divine Milieu*, 60.

23. Teilhard de Chardin, *Divine Milieu*, 61.

24. Søren Kierkegaard, *The Sickness unto Death*, in *Fear and Trembling* and *The Sickness unto Death*, trans. Walter Lowrie (New York: Doubleday, 1954), 44.

25. Pierre Teilhard de Chardin, *Let Me Explain*, trans. Jean-Pierre De-moulin (New York: Harper & Row, 1966), 127 [emphasis in original].

26. Teilhard de Chardin, *Let Me Explain*, 127.

27. Dylan Thomas, "Do not go gentle into that good night."

28. Teilhard de Chardin, *Let Me Explain*, 127 [emphasis in original].

29. Teilhard de Chardin, *Let Me Explain*, 127.

30. This voiceover narration was written by director Jack Arnold.

31. Matheson, *Shrinking Man*, 190.

BIBLIOGRAPHY

Balmer, Edwin, and Philip Wylie. *When Worlds Collide.* Philadelphia: Lippincott, 1932.

Bates, Harry. "Farewell to the Master." http://thenostalgialeague.com/olmag/bates-farewell-to-the-master.html.

Battle, John Tucker. Original script for *Invaders from Mars* (1956), revised September 5, 1950. http://leonscripts.tripod.com/scripts/INVADERSold.htm.

Bethe, Hans. A. *Three Tributes to J. Robert Oppenheimer.* Princeton, N.J.: Institute for Advanced Study, 1967.

Booker, M. Keith. *Alternate Americas: Science Fiction Film and American Culture.* Westport, Conn.: Praeger, 2006.

———. *Monsters, Mushroom Clouds, and the Cold War: American Science Fiction and the Roots of Postmodernism, 1946–1964.* Westport, Conn.: Greenwood, 2001.

Braucourt, Guy. "Interview with Don Siegel." In *Focus on the Science Fiction Film*, edited by William Johnson. Englewood Cliffs, N.J.: Prentice Hall, 1972.

Burroughs, William S. *The Job—Interviews with William S. Burroughs by Daniel Odier.* New York: Grove, 1974.

Campbell, John W., Jr. "Who Goes There?" In *Who Goes There? Seven Tales of Science Fiction.* Westport, Conn.: Hyperion, 1976.

Caute, David. *The Great Fear: The Anti-Communist Purge under Truman and Eisenhower.* New York: Simon & Schuster, 1978.

Clute, John, and Peter Nichols, eds. *The Encyclopedia of Science Fiction.* New York: St. Martin's, 1993.

Credick, Anna. *Fear Itself: Enemies Real and Imagined in American Culture.* West Lafayette: Indiana University Press, 1999.

DVD Savant. Reviews of *Invaders from Mars.* DVDTalk.com.http://www.dvdtalk.com/dvdsavant/s96InvadersA.html and http://www.dvdtalk.com/dvdsavant/s691mars.html.

Edwards, Jonathan. "Sinners in the Hands of an Angry God." July 8, 1741. Available at Christian Classics Ethereal Library, http://www.ccel.org/ccel/edwards/sermons.sinners.html .

Enoch, M. David, and Hadrian N. Ball, eds. *Uncommon Psychiatric Syndromes.* London: Arnold, 2001.

Evans, Christopher. *Writing Science Fiction.* London: A & C Black, 1988.

Farrell, John. *Freud's Paranoid Quest.* New York: New York University Press, 1966.

Fiedler, Leslie. *Love and Death in the American Novel.* New York: Criterion Books, 1960.

Finney, Jack. *Invasion of the Body Snatchers.* New York: Scribner, 1988. First published in 1954 as *The Body Snatchers.*

Fitting, Peter, in Charles Elkins, ed., "Symposium on *Alien,*" *Science Fiction Studies* 7, no. 3 (November 1980): 278–304.

Freeman, Daniel, and Philippa A. Garety. *Paranoia: The Psychology of Persecutory Delusions.* New York: Psychology Press, 2004.

Freud, Sigmund. *Civilization and Its Discontents.* Translated and edited by James Strachey. New York: Norton, 1961.

———. *The Standard Edition of the Complete Psychological Works of Sigmund Freud,* vol. 12, translated and edited by James Strachey. (London: Hogarth 1955): 67–68 [emphasis in original].

———. "The Uncanny." In *The Standard Edition of the Complete Psychological Works of Sigmund Freud,* vol. 17, translated and edited by James Strachey. London: Hogarth, 1955.

Gilbert, G. M. *Nuremburg Diary.* New York: Farrar, Straus, 1947.

Gilmore, David D. *Misogyny: The Male Malady.* Philadelphia: University of Pennsylvania Press, 2001.

Green, Celia. *Lucid Dreams.* London: Hamish Hamilton, 1968.

Hendershot, Cyndy. *Paranoia, the Bomb, and 1950s Science Fiction Films.* Bowling Green, Ohio: Bowling Green State University Popular Press, 1999.

Hite, Shere. *The Hite Report.* New York: Macmillan, 1976.

Hofstadter, Richard. "The Paranoid Style in American Politics." In *The Paranoid Style in American Politics and Other Essays.* New York: Knopf, 1966.

Johnson, William, ed. *Focus on the Science Fiction Film.* Englewood Cliffs, N.J.: Prentice Hall, 1972.

Jung, Carl. *Aion: Researches into the Phenomenology of the Self.* Translated by R. F. C. Hull. New York: Pantheon, 1959.

———. *The Archetypes and the Collective Unconscious.* Translated by R. F. C. Hull. New York: Pantheon, 1959.

———. *Basic Writings.* Edited by Violet Staub de Laszlo. New York: Modern Library, 1959.

———. "Childhood Development and Education." In *The Development of Personality,* translated by R. F. C. Hull. New York: Pantheon, 1954.

———. *Psychology and Religion: West and East.* Translated by R. F. C. Hull. New York: Pantheon, 1958.

Kaminsky, Stuart M. "Don Siegel on the Pod Society." In *Invasion of the Body Snatchers*, edited by Al LaValley. New Brunswick, N.J.: Rutgers University Press, 1989.

Kierkegaard, Søren. *The Sickness unto Death.* In *Fear and Trembling* and *The Sickness unto Death*, translated by Walter Lowrie. New York: Doubleday, 1954.

Landon, Brooks. *The Aesthetics of Ambivalence: Rethinking Science Fiction Film in the Age of Electronic (Re)production.* Westport, Conn.: Greenwood, 1992.

Laura, Ernesto G. "Invasion of the Body Snatchers." In *Focus on the Science Fiction Film*, edited by William Johnson. Englewood Cliffs, N.J.: Prentice Hall, 1972.

LaValley, Al, ed. *Invasion of the Body Snatchers.* New Brunswick, N.J.: Rutgers University Press, 1989.

Lewis, Sinclair. *Main Street.* New York: New American Library, 1961. First published in 1920.

Lorenz, Konrad. *On Aggression.* Translated by Marjorie Kerr Wilson. New York: Harcourt, Brace & World, 1966.

Lucanio, Patrick. *Them or Us: Archetypal Interpretations of Fifties Alien Invasion Films.* Bloomington: Indiana University Press, 1987.

Mainwaring, Daniel. Screenplay for *Invasion of the Body Snatchers.* In *Invasion of the Body Snatchers,* edited by Al LaValley. New Brunswick, N.J.: Rutgers University Press, 1989.

Marx, Karl. *Early Writings.* Translated and edited by T. B. Bottomore. New York: McGraw-Hill, 1964.

———. "Economic and Philosophical Manuscripts of 1844." In *The Classics of Western Philosophy: A Reader's Guide*, edited by Jorge J. E. Gracia, Gregory M. Reichberg, and Bernard M. Schumacher. Malden, Mass.: Blackwell, 2003.

Matheson, Richard. *The Shrinking Man.* New York: Buccaneer Books, 1962.

McConnell, Frank. "Born in the Fire: The Ontology of the Monster." In *Shadows of the Magic Lamp: Fantasy and Science Fiction in Film*, edited by George Slusser and Eric S. Rabkin. Carbondale: Southern Illinois University Press, 1985.

North, Edmund H. Script for *The Day the Earth Stood Still* (1951), revised final draft, February 21, 1951. http://www.scifiscripts.com/scripts/TheDayTheEarthStoodStill.html.

O'Bannon, Dan, and Don Jakoby. Script for *Invaders from Mars* (1986), second draft, December 1984. http://leonscripts.tripod.com/scripts/INVADERSnew.htm.

O'Connor, Flannery. *The Habit of Being.* Edited by Sally Fitzgerald. New York: Farrar, Straus & Giroux, 1979.

Oppenheimer, Robert. "Physics in the Contemporary World." The Arthur D. Little Memorial Lecture at M.I.T., November 25, 1947. Available at http://en.wikiquote.org/wiki/Robert_Oppenheimer.

Plato. *The Republic of Plato*. Translated by Francis MacDonald Cornford. New York: Oxford University Press, 1945.

Rabi, I. I., ed. *Oppenheimer*. New York: Scribner, 1969.

Rawnsley, Gary D., ed. *Cold-War Propaganda in the 1950s*. New York: St. Martin's, 1999.

Rigden, John S. "J. Robert Oppenheimer: Before the War." *Scientific America* 273, no. 1 (July 1995).

Scheib, Richard. Review of *Invasion of the Body Snatchers*. Moria.co.nz.http://www.moria.co.nz/sciencefiction/invasion-of-the-body-snatchers-1956.htm.

Schelde, Per. *Androids, Humanoids, and Other Science Fiction Monsters: Science and Soul in Science Fiction Films*. New York: New York University Press, 1993.

Sobchack, Vivian. *Screening Space: The American Science Fiction Film*. New Brunswick, N.J.: Rutgers University Press, 1987.

Solomon, Marion F. *Narcissism and Intimacy: Love and Marriage in an Age of Confusion*. New York: Norton, 1989.

Steffen-Fluhr, Nancy. "Women and the Inner Game in Don Siegel's *Invasion of the Body Snatchers*." In *Invasion of the Body Snatchers*, edited by Al LaValley. New Brunswick, N.J.: Rutgers University Press, 1989.

Stern, Philip M., and Harold P. Green. *The Oppenheimer Case: Security on Trial*. New York: Harper & Row, 1969.

Teilhard de Chardin, Pierre. *The Divine Milieu: An Essay on the Interior Life*. New York: Harper & Row, 1960.

———. *Let Me Explain*. Translated by Jean-Pierre Demoulin. New York: Harper & Row, 1966.

Telotte, J. P. *Science Fiction Film*. Cambridge, UK: Cambridge University Press, 2001.

Twain, Mark. *Adventures of Huckleberry Finn*. Edited by Henry Nash Smith. Boston: Houghton Mifflin, 1958.

U.S. Atomic Energy Commission. *In the Matter of J. Robert Oppenheimer: Transcript of Hearings before Personnel Security Board, Washington, D.C., April 12, 1954 through May 6, 1954*. Cambridge: M.I.T. Press, 1954.

Wells, H. G. *The War of the Worlds*. New York: Oxford University Press, 1995. First published in 1898.

Whitehead, John W. "*Invasion of the Body Snatchers*: A Tale for Our Times." *Gadfly Online*, November 26, 2001. http://www.gadflyonline.com/11-26-01/film-snatchers.html.

Wingrove, David, ed. *The Science Fiction Film Source Book*. London: Longman, 1985.

Zerby, Stephen A. "Using the Science Fiction Film *Invaders from Mars* in a Child Psychiatry Seminar." *Academic Psychiatry* 29, no. 3 (July 2005): 316–21.

FILMOGRAPHY

THE THING FROM ANOTHER WORLD (1951)

Director: Christian Nyby, with uncredited directorial input by
    Howard Hawks
Producers: Howard Hawks, Edward Lasker
Screenplay: Charles Lederer, based on the short story "Who
    Goes There?" by John W. Campbell Jr., with uncredited writ-
    ing by Howard Hawks and Ben Hecht
Cinematography: Russell Harlan
Editing: Roland Gross
Music: Dimitri Tiomkin
Art Direction: Albert S. D'Agostino, John J. Hughes
Special Effects: John Steward
Visual Effects: Linwood Dunn
Process Photography: Harold E. Stine
Running Time: 87 minutes
Release Date: April 29, 1951
DVD: Turner Home Entertainment
Cast: Margaret Sheridan (as Nikki), Kenneth Tobey (as Captain
    Pat Hendry), Robert Cornthwaite (as Dr. Carrington), Doug-
    las Spencer (as Scotty), James Young (as Lieutenant Eddie
    Dykes), William Self (as Corporal Barnes), Dewey Martin

(as crew chief Bob), Eduard Franz (as Dr. Stern), Sally
Creighton (as Mrs. Chapman), George Fenneman (as Dr.
Redding), Paul Frees (as Dr. Voorhees), James Arness (as
The Thing), Billy Curtis (as The Thing in reduced form).

WHEN WORLDS COLLIDE (1951)

Director: Rudolph Maté
Producers: George Pal, Cecil B. DeMille (uncredited)
Screenplay: Sydney Boehm, based on the novel by Edwin Balm-
er and Philip Wylie
Cinematography: W. Howard Greene, John F. Seitz
Editing: Arthur Schmidt
Music: Leith Stevens
Art Direction: Albert Nozaki, Hal Pereira
Special Effects: Harry Barndollar, Gordon Jennings, Tim Baar,
Dick Webb, Barney Wolff
Visual Effects: Farciot Edouart, Jan Domela, Paul K. Lerpae,
Cliff Shirpser
Technical Advisor: Chesley Bonestell
Running Time: 83 minutes
Release Date: August 1951
DVD: Warner Bros. Home Video
Cast: Richard Derr (as Dave Randall), Barbara Rush (as Joyce
Hendron), Peter Hansen (as Dr. Tony Drake), John Hoyt (as
Sydney Stanton), Larry Keating (as Dr. Cole Hendron), Ra-
chel Ames (as Julie Cummings), Stephen Chase (as Dr.
George Frye), Frank Cady (as Harold Ferris), Haydon Rorke
(as Dr. Emery Bronson).

THE DAY THE EARTH STOOD STILL (1951)

Director: Robert Wise

Producer: Julian Blaustein

Screenplay: Edmund H. North, based on the short story "Farewell to the Master" by Harry Bates

Cinematography: Leo Tover

Editing: William Reynolds

Music: Bernard Herrmann

Theremin Players: Samuel Hoffman, Paul Shure

Art Direction: Addison Hehr, Lyle Wheeler

Special Effects: Melbourne A. Arnold

Visual Effects: Fred Sersen, L. B. Abbott, Lyman Hallowell, Ray Kellogg, Emil Kosa

Running Time: 92 minutes

Release Date: September 28, 1951

DVD: 20th Century Fox Home Video

Cast: Michael Rennie (as Klaatu), Patricia Neal (as Helen Benson), Hugh Marlowe (as Tom Stevens), Sam Jaffee (as Professor Jacob Barnhardt), Billy Gray (as Bobby Benson), Frances Bavier (as Mrs. Barley), John Brown (as Mr. Barley), Lock Martin (as Gort), Frank Conroy (as Mr. Harley), Edith Evanson (as Mrs. Crockett), Patrick Aherne (as a general at the Pentagon), Marjorie Crossland (as Hilda), Glenn Hardy (as an interviewer), Freeman Lusk (as General Cutler), George Lynn (as Colonel Ryder), Millard Mitchell (the voice of a general), Dorothy Neumann (as Margaret), Elmer Davis, Drew Pearson, H. V. Kaltenborn (as themselves) Olan Soule (as Mr. Krull).

INVADERS FROM MARS (1953)

Director: William Cameron Menzies

Producer: Edward L. Alperson Jr.

Screenplay: Richard Blake, from a story by John Tucker Battle

Cinematography: John Seitz

Editing: Arthur Roberts

Music: Raoul Krushaar

Production Design: William Cameron Menzies

Art Direction: Boris Leven

Visual Effects: Jack Cosgrove, Irving Block, Howard Lydecker, Jack Rabin

Running Time: 78 minutes (American version), 82 minutes (British version)

American Release Date: April 22, 1953

British Release Date: March 9, 1954

DVD: United American Video

Cast: Helena Carter (as Dr. Pat Blake), Arthur Franz (as Dr. Stuart Kelston), Jimmy Hunt (as David MacLean), Leif Erickson (as George MacLean), Hillary Brooke (as Mary MacLean), Morris Ankrum (as Colonel Fielding), Max Wagner (as Sergeant Rinaldi), William Phipps (as Sergeant Baker), Milburn Stone (as Captain Roth), Janine Perreau (as Kathy Wilson), Fay Baker (as Mrs. Wilson), Bert Freed (as Police Chief A. C. Barrows), Luce Potter (as Martian Intelligence).

IT CAME FROM OUTER SPACE (1953)

Director: Jack Arnold

Producer: William Alland

Screenplay: Harry Essex, based on a story by Ray Bradbury

Cinematography: Clifford Stine (photographed in 3-D)

Editing: Paul Weatherwax

Music: Irving Gertz, Henry Mancini, Herman Stein

Art Direction: Robert Boyle, Bernard Herzbrun

Visual Effects: David S. Horsley, Roswell A. Hoffman

Theremin Player: Samuel Hoffman

Conceptual Artist: Joseph Hurley

Xenomorph Design: Milicent Patrick

Running Time: 81 minutes

Release Date: May 25, 1953

DVD: Universal Home Video

Cast: Richard Carlson (as John Putnam), Barbara Rush (as Ellen
Fields), Charles Drake (as Sheriff Matt Warren), Joe Sawyer
(as Frank Daylon), Russell Johnson (as George), Kathleen
Hughes (as June), George Eldredge (as Dr. Snell), Bradford
Jackson (as Bob).

THE WAR OF THE WORLDS (1953)

Director: Byron Haskin

Producers: George Pal, Cecil B. DeMille, Frank Freeman Jr.

Screenplay: Barré Lyndon, based on the novel by H. G. Wells

Cinematography: George Barnes

Editing: Everett Douglas

Music: Leith Stevens

Art Direction: Albert Nozaki, Hal Pereira

Astronomical Art: Chesley Bonestell

Special Effects: Chester Pate, Bob Springfield, A. Edward Su-
therland, Barney Wolff

Visual Effects: Ivyl Burks, Jan Domela, Gordon Jennings, Wal-
lace Kelley, Paul Lerpae, Irmin Roberts, Jack Caldwell, Mar-
cel Delgado, Jan Domela

Process Photography: Farciot Edouart

Running Time: 85 minutes

Release Date: August 26, 1953

DVD: Paramount Home Video

Cast: Gene Barry (as Dr. Clayton Forrester), Ann Robinson (as Sylvia Van Buren), Les Tremayne (as Major General Mann), Bob Cornthwaite (as Dr. Pryor), Lewis Martin (as pastor Dr. Matthew Collins), Housely Stevenson Jr. (as General Mann's aide), Paul Frees (as opening announcer and second radio reporter), Charles Gemora (as a Martian), George Pal (as a vagrant listening to the radio), Cedric Hardwicke (as the commentator).

CONQUEST OF SPACE (1955)

Director: Byron Haskin
Producers: George Pal, Frank Freeman Jr.
Screenplay: Philip Yordan, Barré Lyndon, George Worthing Yates, James O'Hanlon, based on the book *Conquest of Space* by Chesley Bonestell (artwork) and Willy Ley (text)
Cinematography: Lionel Lindon
Editing: Everett Douglas
Music: Van Cleave
Art Direction: Joseph MacMillan Johnson, Hal Pereira
Astronomical Art: Chesley Bonestell
Visual Effects: Ivyl Burks, Jan Domela, John P. Fulton, Paul Lerpae, Irmin Roberts
Process Photography: Farciot Edouart
Running Time: 81 minutes
Release Date: April 20, 1955
DVD: Paramount Home Video
Cast: Walter Brooke (as General Samuel T. Merritt), Eric Fleming (as Captain Barney Merritt), Mickey Shaughnessy (as Sergeant Mahoney), Phil Foster (as Jackie Siegle), William Hopper (as Dr. George Fenton), Benson Fong (as Imoto), Ross Martin (as Andre Fodor), Vito Scotti (as Fodor), John

Dennis (as Donkersgoed), Michael Fox (as Elsbach), Joan
Shawlee (as Rosie McCann).

INVASION OF THE BODY SNATCHERS (1956)

Director: Don Siegel
Producer: Walter Wanger
Screenplay: Daniel Mainwaring, based on the *Collier's* maga-
  zine serial "The Body Snatchers" by Jack Finney
Cinematography: Ellsworth Fredericks
Editing: Robert S. Eisen
Music: Carmen Dragon
Production Design: Edward Haworth
Special Effects: Milt Rice, Don Post
Running Time: 80 minutes
Release Date: February 9, 1956
DVD: Olive Films
Cast: Kevin McCarthy (as Dr. Miles Bennell), Dana Wynter (as
  Becky Driscoll), King Donovan (as Jack Belicec), Carolyn
  Jones (as Teddy Belicec), Larry Gates (as Dr. Danny Kauff-
  man), Jean Willes (as Nurse Sally Withers), Ralph Dumke (as
  Police Chief Nick Grivett), Virginia Christine (as Wilma
  Lentz), Tom Fadden (as Uncle Ira Lentz), Bobby Clark (as
  Jimmy Grimaldi), Whit Bissel (as Dr. Hill), Richard Deacon
  (as Dr. Harvey Bassett), Guy Way (as Officer Sam Janzek).

THE INCREDIBLE SHRINKING MAN (1957)

Director: Jack Arnold
Producer: Albert Zugsmith
Screenplay: Richard Matheson, Richard Alan Simmons (uncred-
  ited), based on Matheson's book *The Shrinking Man*

Cinematography: Ellis W. Carter

Editing: Al Joseph

Music: Irving Gertz, Earl E. Lawrence, Hans J. Salter, Herman Stein

Theme Music: Foster Carlin, Earl E. Lawrence

Trumpet Solo: Ray Anthony

Art Direction: Robert Clatworthy, Alexander Golitzen

Special Effects: Cleo Baker, Fred Knuth

Visual Effects: Everett H. Broussard, Roswell A. Hoffman

Special Photography: Clifford Stine

Running Time: 81 minutes

Release Date: February 22, 1957 (New York premiere). General American release: April 1957

DVD: Universal Home Video

Cast: Grant Williams (as Scott Carey), Randy Stuart (as Louise Carey), April Kent (as Clarice), Paul Langton (as Charlie Carey), Raymond Bailey (as Dr. Thomas Silver), William Schaller (as Dr. Arthur Bramston), Frank Cannel (as a barker), Billy Curtis (as Clarice's coworker), Helene Marshall (as a nurse).

KRONOS (1957)

Director: Kurt Neumann

Producers: E. J. Baumgarten, Irving Block, Louis DeWitt, Kurt Neumann, Jack Rabin

Screenplay: Lawrence Louis Goldman, from a story by Irving Block

Cinematography: Karl Struss

Editing: Jodie Copelan

Music: Paul Sawtell, Bert Shefter

Production Design: Theobold Holsopple

Special Visual Effects: Irving Block, Louis DeWitt, Jack Rabin, William Reinhold, Menrad von Mulldorfer, Gene Warren, Wah Chang

Process Photography: Harold E. Stine

Running Time: 78 minutes

Release Date: April, 1957

DVD: Image Entertainment

Cast: Jeff Morrow (as Dr. Leslie Gaskell), Barbara Lawrence (as Vera Hunter), John Emory (as Dr. Hubbell Eliot), George O' Hanlon (as Dr. Arnold Culver), Morris Ankrum (as Dr. Albert Stern), Kenneth Alton (as McCrary), John Parrish (as General Perry), Jose G. Gonzalez (as Manuel Ramirez), Richard Harrison (as a pilot), Marjorie Stapp (as a nurse), Robert Shayne (as an Air Force general), Gordon Mills (as a sergeant), John Halloran (as a Lab Central security guard).

I MARRIED A MONSTER FROM OUTER SPACE (1958)

Director: Gene Fowler Jr.

Producer: Gene Fowler Jr.

Screenplay: Louis Vittes

Cinematography: Haskell Boggs

Editing: George Tomasini

Stock Music: Daniel Amfitheatrof, Hugo Friedhofer, Leith Stevens, Franz Waxman, Victor Young

Art Direction: Henry Bumstead, Hal Pereira

Visual Effects: John P. Fulton

Running Time: 78 minutes

Release Date: October 1958

DVD: Paramount Home Video

Cast: Tom Tryon (as Bill Farrell), Gloria Talbott (as Marge Farrell), Chuck Wassill (as Ted Hanks), Darlene Fields (as Caroline Hanks), Valerie Allen (as Francine), Maxie Rosen-

bloom (as Max Grady), Ken Lynch (as Dr. Wayne), Jean
Carson (as Helen Rhodes), Alan Dexter (as Sam Benson), Ty
Hungerford (as Mac Brody), Robert Ivers (as Harry Phillips),
John Eldredge (as Police Captain H. B. Collins), Peter Bald-
win (as officer Hank Swenson), Jack Orrison (as Officer
Schultz), Charles Gemora (as an alien).

INDEX

ABOUT THE AUTHOR

Michael Bliss teaches English and film criticism at Virginia Tech. His previous books are *Justified Lives: Morality and Narrative in the Films of Sam Peckinpah*; *Doing It Right: The Best Criticism on Sam Peckinpah's "The Wild Bunch"*; *What Goes Around Comes Around: The Films of Jonathan Demme* (coauthored with Christina Banks); *Dreams within a Dream: The Films of Peter Weir*; *Peckinpah Today: New Essays on the Films of Sam Peckinpah*; and from Scarecrow Press, *Brian De Palma*; *Martin Scorsese and Michael Cimino*; *The Word Made Flesh: Catholicism and Conflict in the Films of Martin Scorsese*; and *Between the Bullets: The Spiritual Cinema of John Woo*. Bliss is currently completing his latest book of film criticism.